D0116957

PUPPETS
Methods and Materials

Mallard. Hand puppet by Steven Hansen.

PUPPETS

METHODS AND MATERIALS

Cedric Flower &
Alan Jon Fortney

Davis Publications, Inc.
Worcester, Massachusetts

ACKNOWLEDGEMENTS

Special thanks and appreciation go to Jill Andersen Fortney and her daughter, Rachael Jennifer, who created the puppets found in chapter 1, and who built and/or supervised the building of many others found in subsequent chapters. Justine Hoffman also helped in the making of some simple puppets.

Lolly Marsh, the other half of the Bennington Puppets, offered support and help throughout.

Lara Flower and Marion Appel helped by allowing their hands to be photographed while in the process of building some puppets.

We thank Margo Rose and Allelu Kurten for giving the manuscript a critical read through, and Dave and Ellie Eldridge for providing a place by the sea to do some of the work.

And without the continued and continuing support, and wit, of our editor, Wyatt Wade, this book might still be but a scattering of ideas without strings.

AJF & CSF

Illustration credits

Front cover: String and rod puppets by The Bennington Puppets. Hand puppet by Rachael Jennifer Krygier. Photograph by Alan Jon Fortney.

Back cover: Tyl Eulenspiegel, a five foot shadow puppet made of lexan plastic painted with acetate inks. Created by The Underground Railway Puppets and Actors for their production of *Tyl Eulenspiegel's Merry Pranks*, commissioned by the Boston Symphony. Photograph by Lista Duren.

Silhouettes in chapter 3 and all photographs by Alan Jon Fortney except where otherwise indicated.

All line drawings by Cedric Flower.

Every effort has been made to give credit for sources of photographs. If copyright is claimed for any photographs not credited, the authors will be pleased to correspond with the claimant and to make an appropriate arrangement.

Designer: Janis Capone

10 9 8 7 6 5 4 3 2

CONTENTS

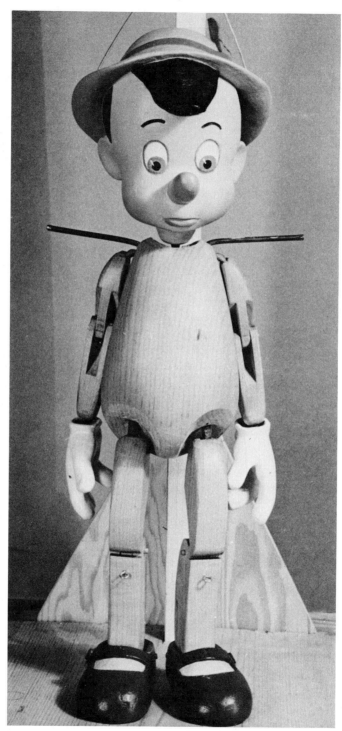

Pinocchio. Copyright © Walt Disney Productions.

INTRODUCTION

Pinocchio began life as a tree. For centuries, puppet making was a wood carvers' art. But just as the cinema has changed the art of acting and the vacuum tube has changed the course of music, so has the petroleum industry altered the state of puppetry. Miss Piggy began as a barrel of crude oil. A puppet of foam rubber such as Miss Piggy looks and behaves differently from one of wood. This book is an exploration of the hundreds of materials available to puppeteers, many made possible by modern science. This book explains how these materials are worked within puppetry and how these materials have broadened the possibilities of the art. The modern puppet maker is an alchemist, with pots and caldrons, transforming syrups and brews into life.

All materials fall into the two categories of natural and synthetic. Until the advent of modern chemistry, things possessed the properties nature directed. Today, we choose materials for their properties of movement or their plasticity. A movable mouth capable of both subtle and obvious expression is achieved with foam rubber, which is not rubber at all, but a flexible foamed plastic made from petroleum. While many natural materials continue to serve well, many have been at least partly replaced by synthetic materials: animal skins by false fur, metals by fiberglass, animal glues by plastic glues. The properties and characteristics of synthetics are infinite. This book serves as a guide to recently developed materials most used in contemporary puppetry, as well as traditional puppetry methods and materials.

Introduction

The purpose of this book is to serve as a source of ideas, an inspiration for you to direct your creativity into the world of puppetry. Puppets and techniques in this book move naturally from easy to intricate. Chapter one offers many imaginative ways to make puppets easily, providing nearly instant fun. All four classes of puppets are covered here—hand, rod, shadow, and string (marionette). Chapter two provides many general puppet construction techniques, plus sections on planning, design, and puppet materials. Clear details of further methods for making hand, rod, shadow, and string puppets are given individually in the following four chapters. A chapter on painting and stages (from simple to complex) and a chapter on puppets in education round out this puppet manual.

History of Puppetry

The birth of puppetry is unrecorded, but history and legend indicate that puppets have won hearts in many cultures for thousands of years. Heroditus wrote, in the fifth century B.C., of marionettes being used in the Egyptian Festival of Osiris, adding that figures animated by strings and wires were of great antiquity. But written history otherwise remained silent on the topic of puppetry until the Roman Catholic Church used puppets to perform Bible tales. By the fifteenth century, elaborate puppet plays were being staged in churches in Europe. Because of its starring role in the nativity scene, the stringed puppet became known as a "little Mary" or *marionette*.

Europe   Italian marionettes traveled as far as England, bringing the tradition of *commedia dell'arte*. The spirit of ancient Roman festivals survived in many buffoon characters including Pulchinella, whose name the English shortened to Punch, as in Punch and Judy.

Puppets appealed most often to common people, but at the turn of the eighteenth century they also became a part of sophisticated plays performed in private salons. Operas were written by well-known composers for puppets.

By now, Europe has a long tradition of giving puppetry serious attention, thinking it worthy of intelligent plays, music and high technology. Puppet plays are more than children's entertainment. Russia, Hungary, Czechoslovakia, and Poland still have huge, well financed state puppet companies.

History of Puppetry

The East

In India, legend has it that the *Adi Nat* ("first puppeteer") was born from the mouth of Brahmin, the Creator. Indian missionaries taught Hinduism with rod and shadow puppets, leaving a religion and puppetry tradition still alive today.

India has all four types of puppets—hand, rod, string and shadow—the last two being the most popular. *Kathputli bhats* ("wooden puppet performers") tell the tales recorded in two 2000-year-old epic poems, the adventures of India's heroes, princesses, lovers and demons.

In Japan, rod puppetry reached its apex with the Bunraku theater. The Bunraku repertoire of twenty plays was written by Chikamatsu Monsaemon, Japan's greatest dramatist, who preferred puppets to human actors because they would give precise renditions of his dramatic intentions. The four-foot-high Bunraku figures are so involved, some of them require three people to operate them.

China, too, has all four kinds of puppets. Some of its shadow puppets are delicate works of art, and Chinese hand puppets are known for being small and finely made.

The Americas

Puppetry in the western hemisphere can be documented back to about 300 A.D. The native American cultures of Mexico and Guatamala produced clay figures with articulated limbs. Hand puppets and marionettes were used by native peoples of the North American woodlands, deserts, and northwest coast. Among the Hopi, the Zuni, and some coastal tribes, puppets still are used in ceremonies.

When Europeans came to the New World, European puppetry came too. Cortes brought a puppeteer to entertain the troops when he came to conquer Mexico in 1519. Punch arrived in Philadelphia in 1742. Puppetry made its way into vaudeville, and by the 1920s Tony Sarg was touring the country with his stringed troupers.

The government gave puppetry a helping hand in the 1930s with a WPA project involving 20 working puppet companies. Three hundred and fifty puppeteers and technicians did 100 shows a week, reaching a collective audience of 40,000.

In the 1940s one little American rod puppet, Charlie McCarthy, achieved a reputation in theater that many a live actor would envy. Edgar Bergen and Charlie McCarthy, along with Mortimer Snerd, Effie Klinker and others, had such an enormous following they had their own radio show—quite an achievement for an essentially visual act.

When television became a viable medium in the 1950s, Kukla, Fran, and Ollie made their debut, followed closely by Howdy Doody

History of Puppetry

Edgar Bergen and this little rod puppet named Charlie McCarthy became so popular in the 1940s they had their own radio show. Photograph by Kim Nielsen for the Smithsonian Institution.

During the 1950s, Howdy Doody was the epitome of American boyishness to the countless children who watched him on television. Photograph by Kim Nielsen for the Smithsonian Institution.

With simple, little, cloth hand puppets she named Lamb Chop and Hush Puppy, Shari Lewis was a popular television puppeteer during the 1960s and 1970s. Photograph by Lee Weiner.

and Shari Lewis's Lambchop. And, of course, The Muppets and Sesame Street characters now teach preschoolers everything from numbers and ABCs to self-esteem.

Puppetry is evolving from a traditional folk art into a respected theater form. It is moving from birthday parties and elementary schools into university theater departments, from market places and street corners into film and television studios. Today, puppetry is used in such diverse work as television commercials, drug rehabilitation projects, and reading and special education programs. It is also earning a place as one of the theater arts, where it is developing discerning audiences, attracting imaginative artists, and facing the greatest artistic challenge in its long history.

In the 1920s, Frank Paris began his nightclub career with the help of his marionettes. This particular marionette is now in the Smithsonian Institution. Photograph by Bruno of Hollywood.

Most puppets, especially simple ones, can be made without using any toxic or dangerous materials. When making more complicated puppets, however, you might need some substances which require careful handling. Great care has been taken in this book to give clear warnings about such substances whenever they are introduced. In order to make these warnings prominent, they are printed in bold face. It is up to you to follow these guidelines to protect yourself.

1. Read warning labels and carefully follow all the warning instructions given by the manufacturers of materials you use. Store dangerous substances in clearly marked containers.
2. Keep children away from all harmful and dangerous substances. Use only materials which are labeled "nontoxic."
3. Avoid direct skin contact with such harmful products as some solvents, inks, and paint pigments.
4. Wear appropriate respirators when working with substances such as lacquer, polyester resins, and polyurethane foam. Respirators vary with regard to the substances they filter.
5. Protect eyes, nose, and mouth when using a flocking gun or when grinding styrofoam or fiberglass.
6. Keep flammable solvents and diluents away from heat, sparks, flame, and lighted cigarettes.
7. Maintain good ventilation in your working area, and keep your work space clean.
8. Have a working fire extinguisher on hand. A class A, B, C fire extinguisher is effective on chemical, electrical, and ash-producing fires.
9. Keep all foods, beverages, and containers out of your workshop if you use hazardous materials.
10. Use a safer alternative if you do not have to use a hazardous substance.

Styrofoam balls are a good source of puppet heads. This one is undercoated and its costume is a white cotton glove, making a most simple puppet.

By giving the same puppet a flowing white robe, it turns into a female puppet. Pin the white gauze cloth over the head to make a ghost hand puppet. Loosely fit a rubber band around two fingertips to give the puppet identifiable hands.

1

EASY-TO-MAKE PUPPETS

Work a few features onto the Styrofoam head, give her a hat and a more elaborate costume, and she becomes Mother Earth from *The Enchanted Forest*. Puppet and photograph by Carol Fisan, Teen Concert Theater.

Puppets are everywhere! Once you tune your mind to puppetry, you will see puppets in dust mops, detergent jugs, milk cartons, and Ping-Pong balls. When Jim Henson saw his mother's green felt overcoat and a leftover Ping-Pong ball, he saw Kermit the Frog. Puppet making is the result of imaginative thinking. More an attitude than an act, it is a way of seeing potential animation in inanimate objects.

The simplest finger puppet is made by "standing" your hand on its index and middle fingers, using thumb and little fingers for arms. By decorating your fingers with gloves, poster paper, pipe cleaners, and Styrofoam balls, you can make an unlimited supply of simple puppets.

Finger Puppets

Animal puppets are just as easy to make. Draw a little pig or bird on poster paper and cut it out. Cut two round holes where their legs would be, and insert your index and middle fingers in the holes for legs. Think of what you could do for a giraffe, rabbit, or elephant.

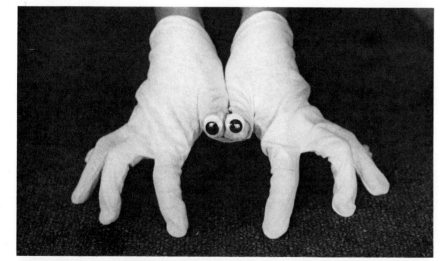

◀ Simple spiders. Put on a pair of gloves and attach eyes to the tips of the thumbs. Connect the thumbs with a rubber band. You can also sew a cotton-filled, pin-cushion-like bulge of cloth on the back of a black glove, decorating the bulge with evil eyes. The bulge is the spider body, the fingers its legs.

◀ Many tiny mice can be created on fingertips. Draw a mouse head and ears on a piece of paper and cut it out. Where the neck would be, cut a band large enough to wrap around a finger. Join the ends of the paper band, and crown your fingertip with the mouse. Or, draw a mouse on a fingertip, and tape cut-out ears to the fingernail. Wrap pipe cleaner around your finger below the second joint for its tail.

Hand Puppets

Put a glove on your hand, and you have a pair of pants for your puppet. Cotton gloves come in several colors, and white ones can be dyed. Make a cardboard or paper cutout of a human head and torso, and tuck it into the "belt" of the pants. Add a tutu for a ballerina.

These ladybugs were made from walnut shells painted orange with a few black spots. Glue short pieces of pipe cleaner onto the shell for antennae. Use different colors to make other bugs.

Mouth Puppets

Mouth puppets are easily made with your thumb and index finger, or with paper bags and plates, egg cartons, mittens, and socks. The simplest of hand puppets are pictured here.

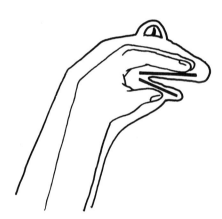

A basic mouth puppet.

To make a frog puppet, fold a paper plate in half. Stitch or staple green felt semicircles to each plate half. Glue or sew pingpong ball halves or pieces of an egg carton to the top half for eyes. Insert fingers into the top and thumb into the bottom half between the felt and the plate.

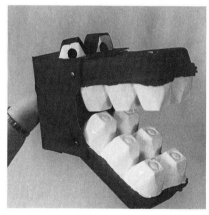

Egg cartons painted green on the outside, and white and red on the egg bumps, make great alligators or dragons.

Cut a piece of paper lengthwise in half. About one third of the way down, fold the paper in so that both folds abut. Grab the paper by the back fold and tape your fingers to the back. The fold will function as a mouth. Use paints, crayons, or felt-tip markers to draw figures on the front of the paper strip. You can also cut the figures out.

Paint the top part of a face on the bottom of a square-folded grocery bag (12# is big enough). Paint the top lip onto the edge of the fold and the bottom lip onto the backside of the bag. Put hand in bag, grabbing fold inside to manipulate the mouth of this bag puppet.

To make the bag look like a pig's head, cut a paper cup as shown, and glue the larger part to the bottom of the bag and the smaller part to the abutting side.

Below left:
Cut a small box in half. Hinge at edge. Paint a face on the box. Insert fingers and thumb into the open ends of the box to manipulate the mouth. Use thimbles for eyes. Paint it grey, make a grey sleeve to fit over your arm, and you have a hippo.

Below right:
Cut a half-dozen egg carton in thirds. Put the egg bumps on the bottom, and you have a small monster. Or put the egg bumps on top and it may be a frog or some creature from outer space. Punch holes in the back, above, and below the hinge (fold), to insert fingers. Just make mouthy heads, or add sleeves for a body. Hands and legs can be added, but they will just dangle (unless you attach rods to them for a modified rod puppet manipulated with your other hand). Make mustaches from rope, ears from felt, hats from paper, and antennae from wire.

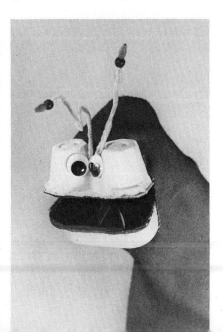

Shadow Puppets

Many of us have experienced the fun of holding up a hand between a light source and a wall, making a variety of shadow shapes. This is the simplest possible shadow puppet. Other shadow puppets frequently are simple paper or cardboard cutouts. Some of the shadow puppets used in eighteenth- and nineteenth-century France were just silhouettes of people, animals, and objects, held between a light source and a transluscent screen. Because the audience sat on the other side of the screen, they saw only the shadows moving on the screen.

To make a simple shadow puppet, cut the outline of a figure out of cardboard and put the cardboard on a stick. For more complicated puppets, make joints in the cardboard figure, using paper fasteners. Attach more rods to control movement of the figure.

Stick Puppets

Another type of puppet that you can make easily and quickly is the stick puppet. The only control in these puppets is the main rod or stick which is used to hold up its body. Some shadow puppets can be considered stick puppets.

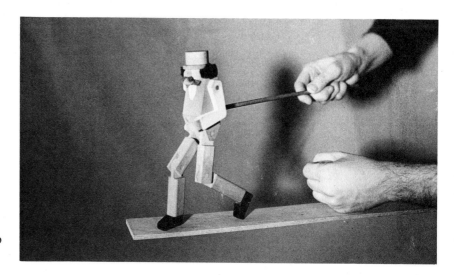

One of the most widely known rod puppets is this folk-art dancing man puppet. By hitting the board, the puppet's legs jump around, and he seems to dance.

As with hand puppets, a wide variety of objects can be transformed to make stick puppets. A little swatch of fake fur, for example, with beads for eyes, put on the end of a pencil makes a little stick puppet you can write with. And balloons, especially pencil-twist balloons, can be twisted and intertwined to make animals and human creatures. Attach a rod (well-rounded so it will not pop the balloon) with tape, and it becomes a stick puppet. Fill it with helium instead, and it becomes an upside-down marionette (controlled from below). Make a gigantic one, and it can be part of Macy's Thanksgiving Parade! Rod puppets, covered in chapter five, are advanced forms of stick puppets.

For an instant stick puppet, take any old teddy bear or doll, and tape, wire, or sew a rod onto it. Attach wire rods to each hand, and you can control the hand/arm movements. Now it is a simple rod puppet.

Rod puppets may also be made from hand puppets, plastic, fruit, cereal boxes, bundles of yarn, carved Styrofoam balls, or one-quart detergent bottles, pictured here.

Stick Puppets

Tennis balls are a good source of puppet heads, as can be seen in these Kurten Puppets.

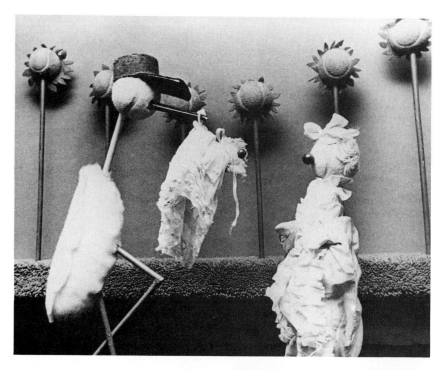

Take a wooden spoon and draw or paint a face in the spoon bowl. Tie a string around the handle to create arms, and attach paper hands to the ends of the string.

A decorated paper plate attached to a stick can also be a very effective stick puppet.

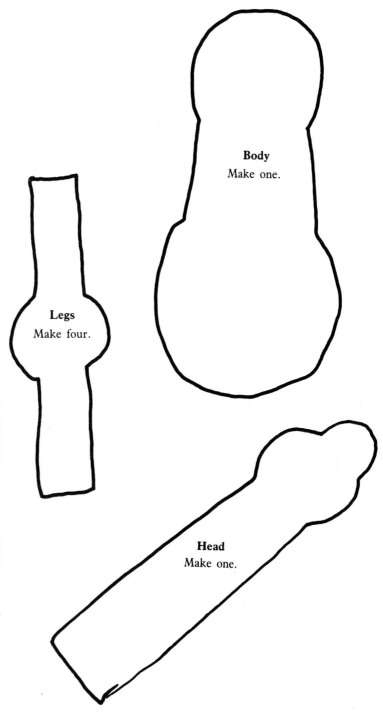

Body
Make one.

Legs
Make four.

Head
Make one.

By tracing these patterns onto sheets of foam rubber, and cutting them out and connecting the parts with contact cement, attaching it to rods and giving it a proper paint job, you have a creditable giraffe.

Marionettes

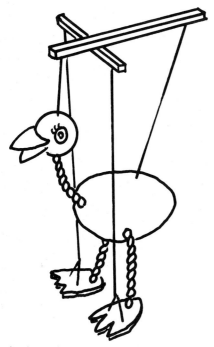

Marionettes are most often quite complicated, but there are a few that can be simply made. By stringing a half dozen Styrofoam balls together, and hanging them from a stick of wood by means of three strings (one string at each end and one attached to the middle), a simple worm puppet can be made. By draping a piece of gauzy white cloth over a Styrofoam ball and hanging it from a stick of wood (one string to the ball and one each to the edges of the cloth) you can make an effective flying ghost puppet with arms.

You can make the shapes of four-legged animals and human beings by knotting lengths of rope together. Hang these from a cross of wood by attaching strings to the head, the body and the arms (or legs) and you have a simple rope human or rope animal marionette. More simply, find a doll whose legs and arms can move freely and use strings to suspend it from a piece of wood. Thus it can be turned into a functioning marionette.

Anything you can hang by strings and move by means of those strings can become a marionette. Your only restrictions are the limits of your imagination.

A simple marionette can be made from rope, styrofoam, wood, and feathers. Plywood feet give this bird weight and motion.

Right:
Get a string of pom-poms, fake fur, and foam rubber and you can put together cuddly little marionettes such as these from Wiggle-Woggle Productions. Photographs by Frank Woodruff.

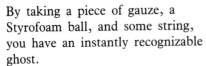

By taking a piece of gauze, a Styrofoam ball, and some string, you have an instantly recognizable ghost.

If you want to get fancy and give the ghosts more distinctive faces and hands, you have a pair like these made by The Puppeteerz.

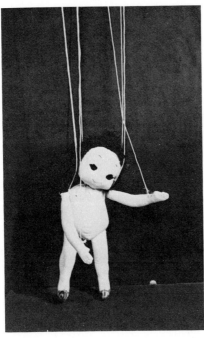

Left:
Many household objects can be the basis of amusing puppets. This coffee pot marionette was made by The Puppeteerz.

Right:
Find a doll, tie strings to its head, shoulders, and hands, and you have an instant marionette.

Simple Puppets

Essentially, puppets can be made out of everything—including a dryer hose. The only limitation is your imagination. These two are from Penny Jones and Company puppets and star in a puppet musical called *The Circus*. Photograph by David Kreindler.

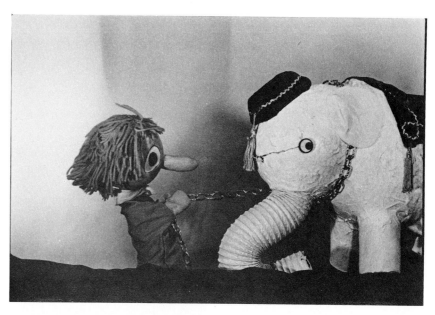

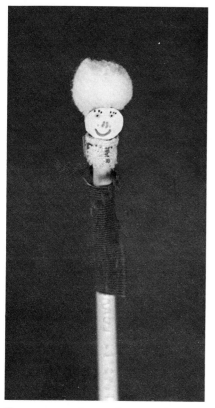

Puppets can be made out of pencils. Just decorate the top with a face, costume, and hair.

Find some cardboard tubes that fit snugly inside one another, paint a face on them, and add a tuft of yarn hair and a costume. This puppet will not only speak for you, she will positively sing!

2

DESIGN,
TOOLS
AND
TECHNIQUES

Bil Baird's Peter and the Wolf
show the kind of caricature that
makes Peter wide-eyed and
unsuspecting while his wolf is
fanged and ferocious. Photograph
from the Bil Baird collection.

Style

Style refers to form, appearance or character in art, to elegance in manners, and to fashion in living. Design is a detailed plan, outline or sketch of a machine or object of art.

In puppetry, style refers to the total impact your puppets have on an audience. Design refers to working out the details of movement and form to be built into a puppet. Samantha Groom's puppet shown here is appealing in style; the design, however, called for mundane items such as a hair curler and an old stocking. Style is the end result; design is the working sketch.

This sweet puppet is built on a plastic hair curler neck. Her face is a nylon stocking, stuffed and stitched by Samantha Groom for The Third Eye Puppets. Photograph by Robert G. Miller.

Puppet Styles

There are four basic styles of puppets: abstract, stylized, caricatured, and realistic.

Abstract

Like abstract art, abstract puppets can be in any combination of shape, form or color. Made of anything you can find, from blocks of wood to Styrofoam beads, these puppets make great use of odd-shaped, otherwise-useless scraps of waste material. Let the material determine what the puppets will look like; these puppets do not always have to represent anything. As long as they can be assembled, lifted and manipulated, they can be abstract puppets.

Bil Baird has an abstract, geometric puppet made of thin tubes which he can manipulate to make endlessly different shapes. The puppet was inspired by Buckminster Fuller, father of the geodesic dome.

Abstract figures can appear human, such as these from Bil Baird's production of *La Caxina*. Photograph by Nat Messik.

These abstract-expressionist faces are made entirely of cloth for the prince and princess in Gem Opera Puppet Company's production of Mozart's *The Magic Flute*. Photograph by Mary Stephens.

Stylized

A stylized object represents something other than itself. A pingpong ball, for example, can represent a clown nose. It is not an exaggeration of a nose, yet it does not look like a nose at all. But in the traditional world of clowns, it has come to be a *new* form that *is* a nose.

Style

Kukla and Oliver "Ollie" J. Dragon (with tooth) are highly stylized hand puppets made by Burr Tillstrom. All the proportions are wrong for the faces, yet Kukla is perceived as a serious, gentle, little man and Ollie as a friendly dragon. Photograph by Linda Schwartz.

Herbert and Lulu, the Hobo Bugs, are stylized puppets with faces and bodies that look nothing like any insect ever seen. Craig Marin and Olga Felgemacher, The Puppeteerz, are their creators. Photograph by Pinwheel Fotos, courtesy of Warner Amex Satellite Series.

Caricatured

Most puppets are in this category. Caricature is the exaggeration of selected movements or features of a puppet.

Jim Henson's Muppets inspired the creation of Detective Snyder and all the other caricatured Kenuppets of Kenuppet Productions. Photograph by Ken W. Bishop.

For instance, Don Quixote may be portrayed as thin and angular while Sancho Panza is round. By making the cranium small, the eyes drooping and the jaw thin and long, Ken Moses made his rod-puppet Quixote a gullible, somewhat mindless and talkative hero and his chubby friend a proper foil. These kinds of exaggerations epitomize caricature.

By carefully selecting a certain emphasis, puppeteers can create their own trademarks that people will learn to recognize as easily as they recognize the work of van Gogh or Mozart.

Don Quixote and Sancho Panza. Photograph by Michael Uffer.

Bil Baird placed the nose high, enlarged the mouth area, and shrank the head area to make the talkative cook and duchess in his production of *Alice in Wonderland*. Photograph from the Bil Baird collection.

These marionettes look at first glance to be quite realistic, especially when they are dressed like their puppeteers. But they are amusing caricatures of the Fool on the Hill puppeteers, with exaggerations of noses and mouths. Photograph by T. C. Eckersley.

William A. Dwiggins with realistic puppet. Photograph by Randall W. Abbott.

Otto Austin makes his puppets half life size (34″ to 42″ tall) to help accentuate the realistic nature of his American Marionette Theater's Specs and Suzie. Photographs by Greg Crawford.

Realistic

Puppets cannot *be* real, but they can *seem* real. Because it is impossible to duplicate reality, strive for the *essence* of real situations, instead. This can be achieved by limiting a puppet's movements. For instance, if just one puppet movement—such as walking or lifting a hand—seems real, the audience will not notice that the puppet is unable to do anything else. The best way to achieve such a semblance of reality is to keep it simple.

The late William A. Dwiggins made a 12″, wood-carved version of himself, exact down to the pipe in hand. His little theater in Hingham, Massachusetts, was devoted in the 1930s and 1940s to creating puppets that looked and moved in a realistic manner.

Even realistic puppets are not exact duplications of the real thing. A good actor will make a realistic impression by slightly exaggerating actions and expressions. This impression would be impossible to create without the willful suspension of disbelief on the audience's part.

In puppet theater, the audience's role is no less vital. The Salzburg Marionettes, for example, perform opera. Since many people go to the opera for the music, first, and the acting, second, the fact that the actors might be a little wooden works to the puppets' advantage. The puppets are only two feet tall, but their job is to perform grand opera miniaturized in all respects except the music. Because performances are done smoothly, audiences *think* the Salzburg Marionettes are exact miniaturizations of live opera.

Although these puppets come from a company called Storybook Theater, Children's Fairyland, they have a very realistic look about them. Photograph by Lonnie Wilson.

Mixing Styles

One of the most important elements of puppetry is consistency of sound, form, and movement within a given performance. You can, of course, mix styles as long as the audience knows what is going on. But if some mechanical abstraction appears in a flowing fantasy for no reason at all, the spell of the performance will be broken.

In short, creating puppets boils down to planning. Part of planning is selecting the puppet's style. The rest of planning comes under *design*.

Planning and Design

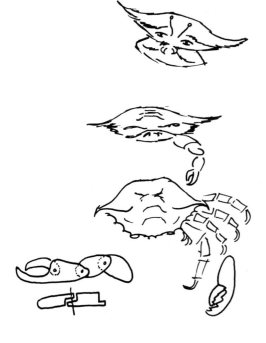

The first step in making a puppet is to do a few quick sketches. These drawings need not be fancy or precise.

Planning puppets involves thinking ahead and working out as many problems as possible on paper before actual construction of a puppet begins. In that most puppets are not very big, most puppet problems will not be very big either. Since it is easier to erase a sketch than to reconstruct a puppet, this is probably the most important stage in creating a puppet.

Begin with a series of questions. What will the puppets' purpose be? Entertainment, skill practice, group activity? What style do I want? Shall I use shadow, hand, rod or stringed puppets? Will they be small or large, simple (for classroom use), or more elaborate (for a professional troupe)? Will they have to fly? Or juggle? Or dance? Must I purchase new materials? Or can I use that box of wooden beads and Styrofoam blocks in the closet?

Planning of complicated, large or trick puppets may be more demanding, but it can still be fun. Consider any limitations on preparation time, construction skills, and the number of people needed.

If you want to work in two dimensions, shadow puppets in front of or behind a screen would work well. If you want your puppet to grab something, use a hand puppet. If you need strong movements of the head and arms, but the leg movements are not important, try a rod puppet. And if you want a puppet to walk in a realistic manner, design a marionette.

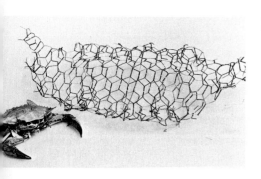

The next step is to select a material to work with that will approximate what you are trying to create or duplicate.

As the puppet is constructed, the details sometimes emerge on their own.

But sometimes, because of the effects desired in production, the whole project must be scrapped, and a new material, foam rubber in this case, introduced. In other words, designing also involves changing your mind.

Research

Research simply means finding out about something. If you want to turn a slinky and two strainers into a cat, you have to know what a cat looks like and how it moves. If you want to make a piece of wood behave like a human being, you will need to know something about human anatomy. If you want your puppet to do something unusual or original, you should know something of anatomy or monsters in order to violate the rules effectively.

Research means going to the cat to find out about catness.

With a little artistic imagination, cat's whiskers can even be made from aluminum foil.

Sewing a slinky to a small strainer with wire inspired this puppet's name—Scratch. Although the idea was simple, Scratch was a difficult puppet to make since the materials were hard to manipulate.

When the task was done, however, Scratch looked the part.

Planning and Design

Every library has books on people, animals, flowers, fantasy figures, other countries, and other times. Decide what your puppet is going to resemble, then look at picture books.

Since puppetry is an art of movement, do not forget to research living examples, as well. This can involve field trips in your backyard or to a zoo, observing people, going to movies, and even watching television. Finally, research involves thought and reflection. Take some time.

As soon as you form an idea about your subject, make a rough sketch. This does not mean the fine art of detailed mechanical drawing. The purpose here is to work out all (or most) of your problems on paper first, not to create a drawing to be hung in an art gallery.

Proportion

Proportion means the relationship between parts. In order to make a rough sketch for a human-like puppet or marionette, it helps to know about human proportions.

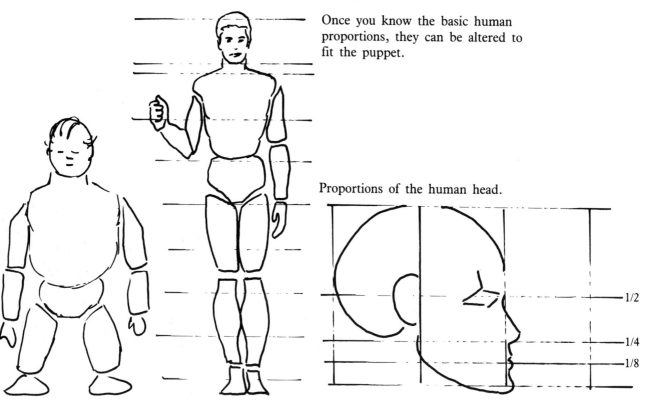

Once you know the basic human proportions, they can be altered to fit the puppet.

Proportions of the human head.

— 1/2

— 1/4

— 1/8

Scale

As there is relative proportion within a face and its features, there must be a relative proportion or scale between the various puppets and set for a given production.

Marionettes usually range from eighteen inches to thirty inches. Some get as small as twelve inches and as large as ten feet and more. Small puppets are easier to handle and are capable of small, delicate, realistic movements. Large puppets are difficult to manipulate but are visible from impressive distances. The reason to select any given size depends on the puppet's purpose, its setting, and even the size of its audience.

After you decide upon the size of a puppet, make every other puppet and prop in the same scale. If a twelve-inch puppet depicts a six-foot-tall person, the scale is twelve inches (one foot) to six feet, or one to six. Thus, all other puppets and objects on the set should be scaled down in the same ratio. If a coffee table is three feet long and eighteen inches tall in reality, it shrinks down to a half-foot long and three inches tall. A dog that is two feet from paws to ears would be reduced to four inches tall.

Of course, you can play with scale to achieve special effects. Variety is natural and to be expected. Don't be a slave to scale, but work within its logic.

Breaking the Rules

Once you understand the rules of proportion in human anatomy, you can effectively break them and experiment with caricatures. By making a skinny body, long legs and arms, and a gaunt, pinched face, you design a teaching puppet of the Ichabod Crane school. By fattening him up, shortening his body and limbs, and adding white whiskers, you create a jolly elf like St. Nick.

Altering the Basic Shape

There are traditional shapes and colorations (see chapter seven) in puppetry that denote different character types. When creating puppets, you must know what these are in order to break the "rules," and you must have good reason to do so. For example, a convex profile depicts a character of action, while a concave profile shows extreme patience. The long, narrow head is visual shorthand for an

The Bennington Puppets needed a monster for the end of its production of *The Time Machine* and resorted to a nine-foot-tall dinosaur body puppet (the puppeteer is inside) to tower over the thirty-inch-tall hero of the show.

Planning and Design

The Soldier from *The Chalk Circle*. Photograph by John Temple.

easy-going type, the round head is jolly, and the wide is combative. A convex jaw joined with a concave forehead shows a person big on action and low on brain power.

The head is basically egg-shaped. Sketch a head and divide it into three bands by drawing one line just above the eyes and another just below the nose. The forehead and crown constitute the top section, the eyes-nose-ears the middle, and the mouth and chin the bottom section. Simple caricature results from altering one of these three sections.

Enlarge a lantern jaw, produce a prominent nose, and the face becomes determined, strong. Exaggerate these features further and the face becomes brutal, villainous.

The nose is a prominent feature on the face. By altering its size, shape and position on the face, you can easily design a caricatured puppet. Placed high on the face, a nose makes the face appear stupid or silly; placed low on the face, it projects an image of reasonable intellect for its subject.

Noses can be beaks, buttons, turned up, pointed down, dominant or practically nonexistent. Daniel Llords used cardboard cartons for heads on all three rod puppets in his production of Stravinsky's *L'Histoire du Soldat* but used round features on the bride's face, molded forms for the mistress's features, and geometric shapes for the diplomat's features.

The Soldier from Underground Railway's production of *The Chalk Circle* has a prominent brow and nose, indicating a personage of strong determination and actions. The mouth, set low in the face almost as an afterthought, indicates a man of few words.

To design caricature into your character, exaggerate the proportions as you sketch the figure. Make the shoulders pinched or as broad and bulky as football shoulder pads. Make the hands huge and expressive, or tiny and delicate. Alter the proportion between the ear and nose, normally the same length, for amusing character changes. The trick is to exaggerate, yet leave the result discernibly human.

The Mistress, the Bride, and the Diplomat from *L'Histoire du Soldat*. Photograph by Turner and Jones.

From a few basic head shapes, a multitude of faces can be made.

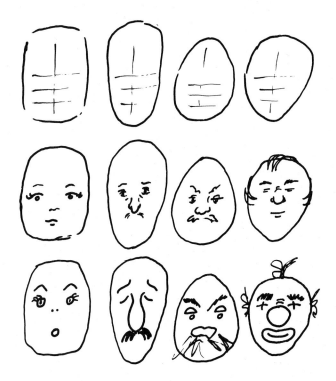

Pieces of Profiles

Examine caricatures frequently used in political cartoons and comic strips. Without directly copying, you can collect a variety of nose shapes, chin shapes and forehead shapes to use in your own sketches and designs.

Make brown paper cutouts of several caricatured jaws, foreheads, or jaw-forehead combinations. Piece these together in any variety of ways, and caricatures will fall into place almost automatically.

Make a sketch of a preferred profile and think about the movements that might be built into the head.

In planning any type and style of puppet, think in terms of simple, geometric shapes. Heads can be squares, rectangles, triangles with the point up, triangles with the point down, trapezoids and cylinders. Eyes, noses, mouths and ears can all be different sizes of the same shapes and proportions.

To make up a design, cut out a number of different geometric shapes of varying sizes and play with them as though they were a puzzle. Even out of simple geometric forms, you can create stylized human-like puppets.

The only limit to varieties in style is your artistic imagination; the only limit to design is your mechanical ingenuity.

Tools and Materials

The construction of many puppets requires the knowledge and use of certain basic tools and materials. Only a few of the tools and materials listed here are needed for making any one puppet. The following list is intended to give readers inspiration and latitude to find even more tools and materials on their own. Such materials as wood, paper, nails, clay, plaster, latex, and hardware are not listed here, being covered thoroughly in those sections which explain their use.

Tools and materials used in some methods of puppet making may pose hazards, as do power tools, sharp instruments, and organic chemicals. Caution is recommended. Bold face type indicates safety information throughout this book.

Tools   Most puppet making is relatively easy and requires few specialized tools. The most important tools are your hands and imagination. Most others can be found in the home, at school, or in any hardware or dime store.

Tool/Equipment	Use
Buckets (clean, disposable, paper painter's buckets); clean metal or glass bowls	To make plaster of paris; for papier-mâché
Cake decorator kit (with an assortment of nibs)	Fill with papier-mâché mash or other malleable material, and appliqué decorations (e.g., eyebrows) onto puppet faces
Chisels (consult advanced books or woodworking teachers for specific items)	Essential for woodworking
Clamps; vices	To hold glued objects until they are dry; to hold work while it is being carved, filed, or sanded
Drills (hand or power)	Many puppets require holes strategically drilled into them
Emery boards (as a substitute for files or sandpaper)	For small sanding projects
Files (flat, round, oval, in many sizes and textures)	Essential for metal and woodworking
Hammers (or fist-size rocks)	For general pounding; breaking molds apart
Holding stand (make one out of a block of wood with a hole in it to	When a vice is unavailable

A hammer is useful for getting puppet heads out of molds.

Tool/Equipment	Use
snugly fit an armature, the frame or base of a sculpture)	
Ice cream sticks; pencils; sharpened dowels; commercial modeling tools	As paddles for modeling, as is, or blunted and beveled
Kitchen knife; teaspoon	For modeling clay, papier-mâché, other soft materials; for prying off lids; prying molds apart; getting into hard-to-reach corners
Paint brushes	For painting (clean after each use); for liquid latex or polyester resins (plan to discard after use)
Pliers	To bend wires; shape metal; general holding; to get eye screws started
Sandpaper (in various grades); emery cloth	Use *wet* emery cloth when working with glass and plastics to make edges smooth
Saws	Cross-cut, back saw, coping saw to cut small pieces. X-acto has a saw blade that fits its No. 5 handle. A band saw for large shaping
Screwdrivers	Useful in prying things apart
Scissors	To cut cloth, paper, cardboard, rubber, foam rubber, aluminum foil; pointed scissors can carve foam rubber; tin snips recommended for medium to heavy-gauge sheet metal
Surform (something between a file and a plane, made only by Stanley Tools)	For woodworking; operates like a food grater, but on wood
Sticks (or clean dowels, pencils, broken slats, and twigs	For stirring
Tape (gaffer's—not useful when wet; masking—not as strong, not useful when wet; other electrical tapes will adhere when wet)	For making boxes for molds (dry); for holding halves of molds together (wet or dry); for attaching lightweight, temporary rods to some puppets

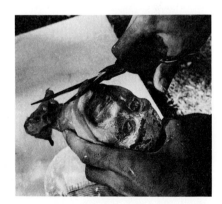

Scissors are all-around useful tools for cutting fabric or foam rubber and even for trimming the seams on a rubber casting.

Tools and Materials

Fabrics

Except in hand and rod puppets in which the fabrics or *costumes* are integral parts, fabrics in puppet construction are used for basic decorations. You can create hair, eyebrows, beards, and other features all from materials found in most fabric stores. Start a scrap box to collect and keep these fabrics.

Although macrame cord is often used as part of a puppet, it can also be used as an entire puppet. Green macrame cord and a pattern for a frog wall hanging in a macrame book inspired the creation of this frog rod puppet. The body is puffed up with a block of Styrofoam, wooden rods are tacked to the hands, and the finished frog looks right in his element.

Fabric	Use
Blankets; old sheets	Anything from a puppet body to a backdrop
Bias tape (or bias trim); seam binding; trim tape	Wrapping burlap boots
Buckram (or buckram tape)	Cut on bias to make eyelashes
Burlap	As a filler for liquid latex; peasant boots; skin for human beings, animals, monsters. Wash before using, to soften it
Cords; white polyester cords; silver and gold cords; braids; borders; piping; macrame cord	Fray and use as hair; macrame a whole rod puppet
Dacron polyester (in many textures—most are shiny)	Fish, serpent, and dragon bodies
Fake fur (in many colors and piles)	As animal hide or in bits and pieces as eyebrows, mustaches and wigs
Felt (in squares or by the yard)	For an animal body; beards; hair; eyebrows (does not require hemming if used as a hand puppet body)
Foam rubber (in sheets, blocks, and shapes)	As a whole puppet; decorative features
Gauze	Ghosts; veils
Handkerchiefs (in many sizes, patterns and colors)	Hand puppet bodies
Interfacing (fuseable, under such names as *Stitch-Witchery* and *Sava Stitch*)	For stiffening insect wings; to make starchy ghosts
Metallic fabrics (some with synthetic gold and silver woven into polyester fabrics; milium lining is stiffer, less elegant looking)	Slinky, shiny rod puppet bodies, such as a wizard's
Mops (wet mops, yacht mops, string dish mops)	Hair pieces; wriggling monsters; oversized paramecia

Fabric	Use
Nylon (or the polyester equivalent found in stockings and pantyhose)	Crumple to make wavy hair; make cuts in it for a droopy mustache; hair; eyebrows
Old socks (from thin to thick and wooly)	Thin green for a serpent hand puppet; fluffy brown for a caterpillar
Old sweaters (or any knitted fabric)	Stuffed with filler and tied at the "neck" for a whole hand puppet
Plaids, prints	Costumes; skins for serpents, monsters
Raffia	Hair (especially if it is disheveled)
Rope (frayed); silk floss; crepe	Hair
Silk	An aristocratic ghost
Sponge (soft, but not wet)	Wrap around glue-covered box for the skin of a monster; pinch, tweak, and model for noses, eye sockets, wrinkles
Taffeta (a shiny, acetate cloth)	Creepy skin for witches and goblins
Terry cloth; stretch terry (in numerous colors)	Cuddly creatures
Trims; braid trims; lace trims; fringes; tassels	Hair; feet
Velvet ribbons (many colors and widths)	Appliqué; glue around neck to add Victorian touch to a woman puppet
Wool (thick—drapes heavily)	Costumes; skin textures; hair
Yarn	Costumes; skin textures; hair

Mops, or strands from mops, make wonderful hair and beards for this Bennington Puppets' wizard.

Perch Puppeteers used exposed gourds with features painted, carved, and glued on for the lead characters of *Princess and the Pea*, while Peter and Tessa, hand puppet chickens, were made from, among other things, old rugs. Photographs by Bob Kelly.

33

Tools and Materials

There is no limit to the materials that can go into puppetry. A sock over a gourd made the head of this Elfking. Cloth, mop strands, pheasant feathers, shells, leather, and seed pods were used to create this rod puppet.

The Patchwork Puppet Company has an alligator made of muslin, acrylic paste, acrylic paint and foam rubber, and an octopus that combines velour and foam rubber (for stuffing). The Jester is made of the same materials as the

alligator, while the bunny, dog and chicks combine fake fur and foam rubber. The fish is a foam rubber form covered with cotton cloth and decorated with netting and satin. Photograph by Rolland R. Meinholtz.

Adhesives In constructing your puppets, you will find many uses for glues. In addition to attaching certain features, such as eyes or hair, glues also strengthen joints using eye screws, nails and screws. Because the bond between the object and the glue is usually stronger than the cohesiveness of the glue itself, keep the layer of glue film-thin. Too much glue actually weakens the bond.

Use caution with glues. Some contain potentially harmful substances, and others bond in a dangerously short time.

Natural Adhesives

Used since time immemorial, natural glues deteriorate over time, but they are usually safe. Store-bought natural glues often have preservatives, such as oil of cloves, formaldehyde, or arsenic, not all of which are safe. Read the labels to be sure.

● Vegetable glues, such as gum arabic, mucilage, wheat and soybean paste, are the weakest of the natural glues. Wallpaper paste comes under this category. Mixed with a little hide glue, vegetable glues are fine for papier-mâché.

● Casein, derived from milk, forms the basis of cheese, certain plastics and a frequently used glue: Elmer's. It will wash out of clothes and off hands when still wet, but not after it is dried. It can be used on all porous and semiporous materials and dries within half an hour.

● Animal glues, derived from blood, albumin, hide and sinews, can be bought as powders or flakes. Animal glues have to be heated, mixed and cooled unless you buy them ready-mixed as hide glue. **The commercially available hide glue contains thiourea, which is harmful if swallowed, has a long setting time, but is very strong.**

● Natural rubber and contact cements never quite dry; they bond objects together by remaining sticky. The most effective way to use them is to coat both surfaces, *allow to dry* to the touch, and then join. This takes a minute or two with rubber cement, and from ten to forty minutes with contact cement. **Because they give off toxic fumes when drying, use only in well-ventilated areas.**

There are other natural adhesives, but they are not generally used in puppetry.

Synthetic Adhesives

● Vinyl and polyvinyl acetates (PVA) are often referred to as *white glue* and can be used in the same way as Elmer's glue.

● Synthetic contact or impact cement is made with neoprene and, like its natural equivalent, should be used with adequate ventilation only. It works the same way as rubber cement.

● Carpenter's glue, a synthetic glue with qualities similar to hide glues, is fast-setting (30 minutes, full cure overnight), and can be used for the same projects as animal glues, casein, and PVA.

● **Airplane glue, available in tubes, contains acetone and butyl acetate, and should be kept away from heat, sparks, open flame and children. It is a quick-drying glue used by model builders.**

There are instant drying glues on the market under the names Super Glue, Krazy Glue, and Gluematic, which are extra-strong, extra-fast drying. **Because these instant glues contain cyanoacrylate ester and bond in seconds, you can inadvertently bond your fingers together and irritate your eyes with the fumes. They are not**

Tools and Materials

recommended for children. Wear a respirator when necessary with other synthetic glues and avoid skin contact.

Compatible Glues and Materials

Adhesives should have a composition similar to that of the item which is being glued. To use an appropriate adhesive, follow this chart. The glues in the left-hand column will stick to the materials listed at the right.

Glue	Material
Nitrate based adhesives; acrylic based cements; epoxy; synthetic rubber.	Plastics
Natural rubber cement; butyl, polysulfide, neoprane, and nitrile rubbers.	Rubber
Animal glue; casein glue; vinyl and polyvinyl acetates; epoxy.	Wood
Epoxy; solder.	Metal

Modeling and Carving

Modeling is the process of shaping and forming a malleable substance into an object, using paddles, sticks, knives or fingers. Although clay is the most commonly used substance in modeling, there is no reason to exclude papier-mâché, cloth, dough, plastic wood, chicken wire and foam rubber. Aluminum foil, for example, can be formed into a face; metal screening can be formed into bodies. Many materials found at home can be manipulated, bended, molded or formed into puppets, parts of puppets and scenery.

Carving in wood is the best method for making quality puppets that endure. One may also carve in Styrofoam, foam rubber, clay, wax and soap. Advocates of the art claim anyone who can sharpen a pencil by hand or peel a potato can learn to carve.

The following is a list of materials that are used to model and carve puppets.

There are two kinds of clay. The original clay, not recommended for puppetry, is water based and is used in pottery and ceramic sculpture. When dried and fired in a kiln, it becomes stone hard. The other kind of clay, *modeling clay*, is linseed-oil based. Its most common use in puppetry is in modeling heads.

Since puppet heads are small and viewed from a distance, the features have to be exaggerated to be seen. If you work with the armature in a base, make sure the puppet does not end looking *up* at you, which can easily happen if you work seated at a table. If the puppet is to be a marionette, it should look out at you, face to face. If it is to become a hand or rod puppet, it must look slightly down, because its stage is slightly above the audience. Even with puppets, "eye contact" is important. You do not want the star of the show staring at the ceiling, ignoring its audience.

A head for a marionette is essentially the same as that for a rod or hand puppet of the same size. For the neck, however, a dowel armature is too small. When the sculpted head is complete with details, add a clay neck. A marionette generally requires a neck with a solid rounded bottom because it fits into a neck cavity. Hand and rod puppets need an open-bottomed neck so that fingers or a rod may be inserted into the hollow head. If you include such things as moving eyes and mouths, design the mechanics first and sculpt around them.

Clay

On left is a finished head, on right is a piece of roughly shaped clay on a dowel to be used as an armature. The vertical line in the clay locates the center of the face, and the horizontal lines divide the face into thirds for the (1) crown and brow, (2) the eyes, nose, cheeks and ears, and (3) the mouth and chin.

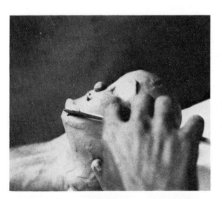

Although a modeling tool can be bought, a sharpened dowel or pencil and a common kitchen knife will suffice for most modeling jobs.

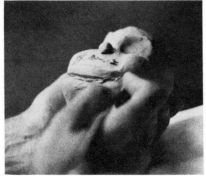

Start by building up masses. With your thumbs, push in where the eye sockets are to go and build up the mass of the forehead above it. Then build up the masses of the cheeks and chin.

Even without adding the details of hair, ears, eyes and nose, a recognizable human face will emerge quickly. By adding an exaggerated nose and chin to this head, nine-year-old Lara Flower easily created a caricature of a witch's head.

Modeling and Carving

It helps to have an illustration of the puppet you are going to make or a sketch of some kind. By using it as a guideline, you can continually check your progress against it.

Because a human face moves, expression comes from movement. But because a puppet face is immobile, movement must be suggested from exaggerated shapes. If you want the puppet to have movable eyes, it would be wise to sculpt them large. If you want a movable mouth, consider how pronounced you want it to be. Cleverly placed shadows can actually make a puppet's face seem to change expression. But do not go overboard on details. Keep the puppet's face clean and simple. Lots of little details, such as warts, wrinkles and scars, clutter up a puppet's face.

Hands, feet, and shoes are easily made of clay. Because most puppets' bodies and limbs are hidden under their costumes, they are not usually modeled in clay. However, for exposed bodies and limbs, modeling clay is a preferred material.

There are many commercially available modeling materials. Modeling dough is a plastic composition that is as soft and pliable as clay. Objects made from modeling dough become hard and relatively permanent when dry and can be finished with oil paints or tempera. Cellulose-based modeling and casting compounds are also available. Their commercial names are Sculpey and Sculptamold, respectively. They come in powder form, model like clay, and become plaster hard.

To simulate a wood carving without all the work and skills involved in working with wood, carve modeling clay (not potter's clay) with sharp carving knives, gouges, chisels and scrapers. Temperature

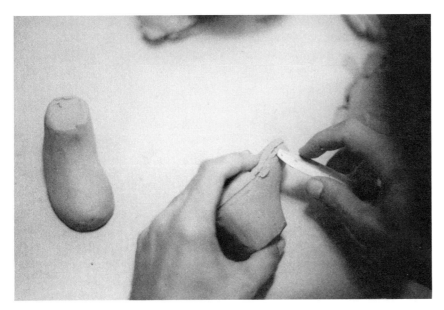

affects clay; keep the clay chilled. Use an armature so the heat from your hand does not warm the clay and make it too flexible. One great advantage of using clay as a carving medium is that if you make a mistake and slice away too much, you can model the clay back into place and, after it is rechilled, carve it again. Since clay is not suitable for a finished carving, make a plaster cast of the clay carving and reproduce it in plastic wood or another permanent medium (see molds and casting, in this chapter).

Another, perhaps surprising, medium for sculpture is dough. Dough achieves a clay-like consistency and character and can be used much as clay is. It can be formed, braided, coiled, sliced, pierced, and pressed into molds. Dough can be used to make small objects, such as a hand, or large ones, such as a piece of scenery. After shaping, the salt dough should be placed in an oven to heat.
   One recipe that has come to our attention calls for

> 4 cups of flour
> 1 cup of salt
> 1 1/2 cups water
> 1 or 2 tablespoons vegetable oil. The oil makes
>   the mixture pliable.

First mix salt and flour in large mixing bowl; then add 1 1/4 cups water. Add oil and remaining water while kneading for seven to ten

◄
Whenever modeling in clay, you are likely to do some carving along the way.

▲
Make certain the object carved or modeled will serve the purpose for which it is intended. An armature in a clay model makes it easier to form a mold around the clay.

Modeling in Salt Dough

minutes. At this point the dough mixture is ready to be sculpted.

For the least warping, bake salt dough sculptures in a 150 degree oven for about eight hours. If you are in a hurry, a 200 degree oven for two hours or a 350 degree oven for one hour will do. Poke holes in the sculpture with a pin to allow air to escape. If puffing persists, make more pin holes and reduce the heat by 25 degrees.

It is best to use a thin layer of dough to avoid warping and puffing. When making a sculpted figure or head, use an armature of aluminum foil for the basic shape and cover it with the dough.

If you use the dough for scenery or props and if the theatrical production is of limited duration, you might get away with using unprotected baked dough. Because it is a soft substance and easily broken, especially in energetic puppet shows, it is wise to give the finished and baked sculpture a skin of Pariscraft or laminated papier-mâché. A layer of polyurethane or clear shellac helps keep moisture out of finished pieces.

The great advantages of salt dough are that its ingredients are readily available and quite inexpensive, it is fast to work with, and details can be added even during the baking process. And baked salt dough is light, a valuable quality in puppetry.

Papier-mâché Mash

Also known as papier-mâché mush, this is very shredded paper mixed with glue and water to create something similar to modeling clay. The commercial equivalent, Claycrete, has all the qualities of papier-mâché, except it comes in a dry form, mixes with water, and is ready to model in fifteen to twenty minutes.

Soak the paper overnight in a pail of water to loosen up the fibers. Use clean newsprint or paper toweling, depending on the strength needed. Newsprint is the stronger of these two. Brown wrapping paper is stronger still, and makes a good final layer.

The ink used to print newspapers contains toxic chemicals and is petroleum based. Newsprint paper which has never been printed on is therefore recommended for use in making papier-mâché.

When fibers are totally saturated, shred the soaked paper with your hands. When the paper is shredded to a mush, drain it with a collander, sieve, or screen and place in a mixing bowl, to be mixed with glue.

The glue is a combination of equal parts of wheat paste, carpenter's or hide glue and whiting (a filler that takes the sheen off organic glues), diluted to the consistency of milk. A little oil of cloves will help preserve the glue, especially in warm weather, but it is cheaper to make only what is needed for a given project.

Papier-mâché mash for puppet hands.

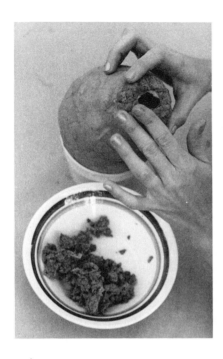

Work a little of the glue mixture into the paper mush with your fingers until it is the consistency of soft modeling clay, only a bit more crumbly.

Papier-mâché mash functions much like modeling clay, except you cannot use much or make anything very thick with it. Because of its long drying time, try to limit thickness to about one-quarter inch. Papier-mâché mash is good for making small parts of a puppet, such as the hands.

This mash can take from one to four weeks to dry, depending on humidity, temperature and thickness. It is more malleable but less strong than laminated papier-mâché. Reinforcements of wood doweling, wire, and a papier-mâché skin are recommended.

Laminated Papier-mâché

The best known of papier-mâchés, laminated papier-mâché is made simply by soaking small pieces of paper in glue and laminating layers of paper one over the other. Although some linen papers still exist, most paper is basically wood fiber and absorbs water. This makes it ideal for papier-mâché.

Clean newsprint is the best material for papier-mâché because it is almost universally available, highly absorbent, and results in a substance of reasonable strength. Brown wrapping paper is less absorbent, but it is stronger than newsprint and is usually used on the final layers for added strength. Paper toweling is the most absorbent of the three, but it has the least body strength.

If you use newsprint for the first layer, use paper toweling for the

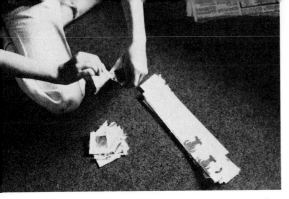

Paper should be torn, not cut, for papier-mâché.

Applying glue-dipped paper.

second. If you alternate two kinds of paper it is easier to keep track of how many layers you are applying.

Tear the paper into 1″ (2.5 cm) squares (smaller for small work and details, larger for bigger projects). Do not cut the paper with scissors; a ragged edge is preferable because it will not show as much as a cut edge. Tear whatever pieces you can reasonably expect to use for a given project *before* starting to work with glue.

To cover a clay model of a puppet's head, gather the three kinds of paper and a bowl of the glue mixture. Dip squares of paper into the glue and apply to clay head. Do not overlap them (unless bumps and ridges are desired in the finished skin); abut them. Completely and evenly cover the entire surface of the head. Overlap the abutments of the first layer with the squares for the second layer, as a bricklayer would. If details are not essential, use the brown wrapping paper squares as a final skin for added strength.

The number of layers you make will determine the strength of the finished product. Eight to ten layers, plus two or three of brown paper, is good for most objects that have to stand up on their own (after the clay head is cut out of it). Add a day to the drying time for each layer after seven. If you are going to use the papier-mâché only as a skin for an object made of chicken wire or tissue mâché, three or four layers will suffice.

Tissue Mâché

This is the speed demon of papier-mâché since it dries in only a few hours. It is particularly useful in making large masses quickly, and, being extraordinarily light, it is good for large puppets. Because tissue paper is flimsy and disintegrates easily when wet, a certain amount of practice will be required to master the technique. The ingredients are tissue paper and a wide-mouth bowl of the glue mixture. Have a pail of clean water available for rinsing and a towel for drying hands.

In working with tissue mâché, you need to start with an armature, preferably of chicken wire, cut to the approximate shape of, but smaller than, the finished product. Form it into the shape of the desired finished product. The armature must be on a stand so that both your hands are free to work with the tissue mâché.

Cut a pile of 1′ (.3 m) square pieces of tissue paper. Corrugate, or fold, a square of tissue paper, but *do not crease it*. Make 2″ (5 cm) folds to obtain a rippled effect, like ribbon candies. Do one at a time, but work quickly.

While holding the shape in one hand, rapidly and lightly coat the top of it with a thin layer of diluted glue mixture. Flip it over and coat the other side. Do not saturate the tissue paper with diluted glues because the tissue will disintegrate. You must maintain the paper's stiffness in order to build up mass by trapping air in the folds of the light paper.

Too much glue will cause the paper to collapse under the weight of water. Use just enough glue to adhere one layer onto the previous layer.

Very carefully lay the mass of corrugated tissue on the armature. Do not compact it! Gently curve it into the armature. Do not overwork the tissue, or it will collapse. After covering the entire armature, add more layers until the desired mass is reached.

As you add layers of the rippled tissue, gently form it. Do not smooth the surface, but nudge it into shape. Tissue mâché has the

4

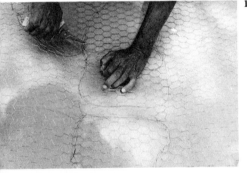

1

Modeling in tissue mâché.

7

5

6

2

3

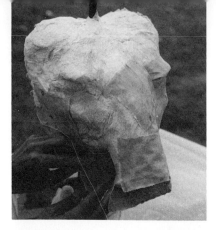

consistency of cotton candy and can be shaped, curved, indented, formed—sculpted, in short—easily. One to four inches (2.5 cm to 10 cm) is the optimum thickness.

Because tissue mâché is a soft surface and not durable enough for a finished puppet, another skin is required. Laminated brown papier-mâché, glue-soaked burlap, cotton or felt may be used. Celastic, a commercially available resin-impregnated cloth, may be used.

The Celastic skin, which hardens to the firmness of shoe leather, is the final shape. The Celastic is cut open, the tissue paper and wire armature removed, and the Celastic is put back together. In this case, the Celastic skin was then covered by a shimmery, grey, stretch terry cloth which seemed very appropriate for a small elephant. An explanation of how to cast Celastic will be found later in this chapter.

The great advantage of the three types of papier-mâché is that they are inexpensive. Additionally, they all use materials that are nontoxic and are therefore safe for children. The finished surfaces can be sanded, painted, and easily repaired. They are also light—a very important quality for puppets. Their disadvantage is, except for tissue mâché, the long drying time required after construction.

Cloths and Hardware Cloth

Modeling with cloth really means modeling with chicken wire and covering it with cloth. Hardware cloth is not cloth, but a stiff wire mesh. Forming three-dimensional objects out of cloth is called tailoring, and many tailoring techniques are applicable when working in this medium. Hardware cloth requires that you work out your pattern, complete with tucks, pleats and stitching, in advance. **Be sure to handle hardware cloth carefully; you can easily cut yourself with it.** Chicken wire, on the other hand, is lighter and, if you make mistakes in your pattern, it is easier and malleable enough to make changes and manipulate it into another shape.

After you create a basic shape, cover it with a cloth skin. Choose a natural, absorbent material that can be cut up into strips and swatches, soaked in the glue solution and layered onto the wire. If you use burlap, do not buy finished burlap that is chemically treated, because it is less absorbent than raw burlap. Apply several layers.

For a final layer, the fabric you choose will depend on the effect you want to achieve in the finished "skin." Use the same fabric used for previous layers, or try cotton or wool for variations in surface texture.

You may want to give the final layer some additional thought and tailor the fabric to fit since it will be the finished visible skin of the puppet.

There are several commercially available modeling cloths that you can use. Celastic has a leather-hard consistency and can be shaped and modeled. **Celastic is easy to work with, but not recommended for young children because an acetone solution is needed to make it malleable.** Apply it directly to a chicken wire sculpture. Both Crea-Gauze and Pariscraft are plaster-impregnated cloths, such as those used in plaster casts. They can be sculpted and modeled around an armature and dry in minutes to the consistency of plaster. The finished surface can be sawed, drilled, sanded, filed and decorated with crayons and paints.

Another way to sculpt with cloth is with a nylon stocking, stuffed with cotton or polyester batting. Simply take stitches with a needle and thread, and pucker the nylon into noses, mouths, cheeks, eyes and other shapes.

This magician's face is a nylon stocking, stitched and tucked to form the features. Created by Samantha Groom of The Third Eye Puppets. Photographed by Robert G. Miller.

Foam Rubber

The wonderful quality of foam rubber is that, while being stiff enough to stand on its own, it is very flexible. This quality is very desirable in hand puppets, especially those who like to talk. The Muppets are foam rubber.

Foam rubber is made of both synthetic and natural rubber. It comes in blocks, sheets, pillows, and hassock shapes, and is available in a variety of densities.

Because sculpting in foam rubber is fairly advanced, you should make a model of the desired finished product. A paper pattern may be made from the model and redrawn on the foam rubber. Draw the profile on the side of the foam rubber block, and the front view on the front of the block.

Use a sharp knife or an X-Acto knife for rough cutting. Compress the foam rubber while carving to produce a clean edge. For final shaping and detail work, make very small snips with a pair of scissors. Folding or squeezing the foam rubber may help when you make delicate cuts and indentations.

Foam rubber pieces are carefully glued together with contact

Clay model for foam rubber puppet.

Modeling and Carving

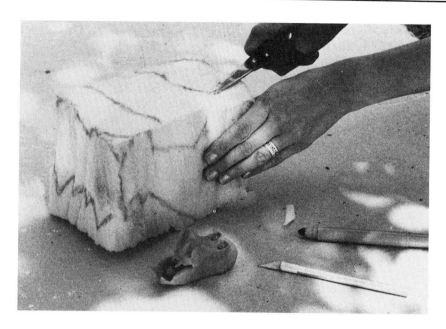

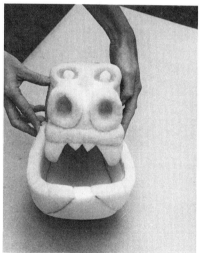

cement. Contact cement adheres instantly and can be pulled apart only with difficulty. Uneven cuts and rough edges may be repaired with contact cement.

For a smooth, rubbery finish, paint liquid latex on the foam rubber, or brush on some latex paint to preserve its foamy texture. You may also cover the foam rubber by attaching tailored cloth "skins" with contact cement. It is important to use flexible paints, glues, and skins, since the foam rubber, itself, is flexible. **Use caution in handling contact cement and liquid latex.**

Ludwig the Lion is a foam rubber version of a Simplicity pattern for a cuddly lion pillow. The creator, Marion Appel, followed the pattern instructions and connected the seams with contact cement. The mane is made from a rag mop, the pince-nez from a coat hanger and the pince-nez ribbon from cobbler's thread macramed with simple knots.

Styrofoam   This expanded plastic is so easy to work with that it can almost be carved with fingernails. But for a smoother surface, sharp knives are recommended. Styrofoam comes in different densities, resulting in differently textured finished carvings. Styrofoam can be "heat carved" with a hot knife or soldering iron. It will melt like butter. **Do not heat carve urethane foam, however. Toxic gasses would be released.**

For a simple project, start with a two or three inch (five to seven cm) Styrofoam ball or eggs and a small sheet or block of Styrofoam. Carve ears, nose, and lips out of the sheet or block, and glue to the balls or eggs. (The features stay more secure during gluing if you push toothpicks into both feature and head.) Eyes can be carved and glued on or carved directly into the head. To make a hand puppet, push your index finger in where the neck should be.

Styrofoam sheets may also be glued together to make blocks. Some glues dissolve styrofoam, so test a small sample. The kinds of heads and faces carved into styrofoam sheets are limited only by the size of the block and the amount of imagination.

As with any carving, draw a profile on the side of the block and the front view on the front as was done on the foam rubber. As you carve out the profile, the flat surface upon which you drew the front view will be carved away. Redraw it when you get half the profile carved (say, from the tip of the nose up) to help keep the perspective. Finish carving profile and redraw bottom front view. Remember these drawings are only guidelines. Redrawing helps refine the process. Mistakes happen easily in this soft material, but it helps to remember that mistakes often lead to new and better ideas.

Styrofoam is not a very sturdy substance, but it is very easy to carve and shape with knives, files (rasps) and Surform tools (a kind of grater made for woodworkers). Styrofoam can be gessoed and painted or be given a skin of papier-mâché, glue-saturated cloth, or Celastic. A commercially made "skin" for styrofoam can be purchased at sculpture supply stores. Gesso is a brand of plaster-in-glue mixture

This gypsy lady was sculpted out of foam rubber. The skin of the face and hands is unadorned, unpainted foam rubber.

Ludwig the Lion. Foam rubber, made from a sewing pattern.

used to prime painters' canvases to hide the canvas texture. You may also make casts out of plaster or liquid latex to reproduce the Styrofoam in a more durable material.

Styrofoam has one interesting quality that is advantageous when covering it with laminated papier-mâché: it dissolves in solvent. Once enough layers of papier-mâché are applied and dried, suspend the object over a bowl of acetone or some similar solvent inside an upside-down paper bag or airtight box. When the Styrofoam dissolves, it will leave the object hollow. Since about the only thing lighter than Styrofoam is air, this is not done for reasons of weight. But if you wanted to create movable eyes or a movable mouth, the puppet head would have to be hollow. **Use extreme caution with solvents and solvent vapors.**

Carving Stone

When mixed with water, this powdered compound forms a thick slurry that can be poured into a milk carton, shoe box, or other suitable shape. It hardens into a substance that is as carvable as soap. Store it in an airtight container, such as a closed plastic bag, and it will remain carvable for months.

Carving stone dries to the hardness of casting plaster and is permanent and weatherproof. The substance is available under such commercial names as Crea-Stone and Karvastone. It can be worked with spoons, knives, gouges, hooked scrapers and rasps. Sets of carving tools are also available. The finished product is too heavy for puppetry, so a casting made from it in a lighter material is recommended (see Molds and Casting in this chapter).

Wood

If you decide to work in wood, it helps to have patience and a good disposition; the skills and knowledge of woods and tools take a lifetime to acquire. Balsa wood (not to be confused with balsam) almost does not qualify as wood. It is very easy to carve, very soft, and lightweight. It is not recommended for a finished puppet carving, however, because it is so easily damaged during use.

Wood puppets tend to be heavy. For heads, hands and feet, close-grained hardwoods and fruitwoods are recommended. Soft woods, like pine, are suitable for bodies and limbs. The puppet Pinocchio's name is Italian for pine-eye (i.e. knothole). If hardwoods are not readily available, pine will do for all parts of the puppet. It has two advantages: it is softer, and it is almost universally available.

For carving harder woods, you will need gouges (front-bent and back-bent), firmer, fluters, a small mallet, a saw, a plane, a small

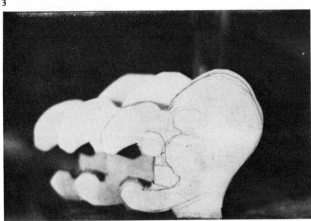

needle file for finishing work, and a variety of files, rasps and sandpapers.

When carving, always work with a guide—either a full-sized clay model or a full-scale drawing, front and profile. If you choose to make a drawing, transfer it, freehand, onto the block of wood to be carved. The easiest way to form the profile is to cut it out with a band saw or coping saw.

If a block of wood is unavailable, planks or pieces may be used. These planks or pieces can be laminated together to form a solid piece about the desired width of the puppet. A hide glue is recommended for the lamination and the piece should be placed in a vice and allowed to dry for at least a day. When the glue is dry, the piece may be carved.

The carving should always be held firmly in place. Leave enough extra wood in your "blank" profile to keep the carving in a vice. If there is no excess wood on the piece, attach a block of wood, with screws, to the base to form a stand that can be inserted into a vice.

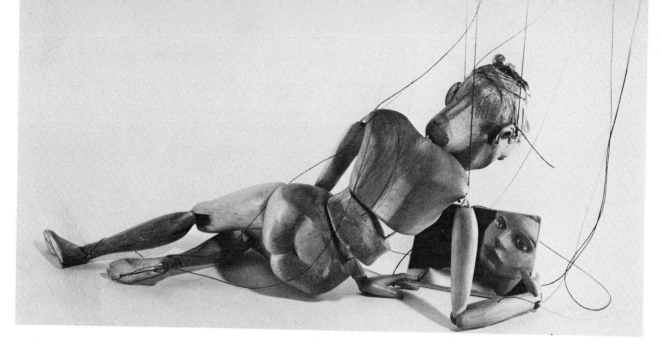

Very few puppeteers learn enough about wood and wood carving techniques to make it a fine art, but the late William A. Dwiggins was one. This foot-high figure has all the classic grace of shape, poise, and movement of many a marble statue.

Wood is Weak Along Grain

Glue in Peg

Wood is weak along the grain. Wooden noses or necks may break. A glued and pegged nose is one solution.

Using gentle taps on the mallet and chisel, start peeling away wood not needed in the profile.

When you have roughed out the "blank" profile, place it in a vice and start forming the shape of the figure. **When sawing, carving, cutting or chiseling, cut away from yourself. Always remember where your fingers are in relation to sharp edges. Work slowly. Work carefully.**

Learning to work with the grain is the most important part of carving. It is best to work in the direction of the grain as much as possible, since cutting across the grain splinters the wood. When carving a puppet head, the direction of the grain should be from top to bottom, vertical to the face. Wood is weakest along its grain, so be aware to avoid having the puppets' noses and fingers fall off.

By nature, wood is a bulky, angular material. To accentuate these qualities and to bring out the grain, carve flat planes and use geometric curves and sharp, severe cuts. A plane renders sharper outline and stronger shadows than a curved surface. Where possible, carve smooth, distinct lines, and avoid sanding, which tends to smooth away the character of a carved finish.

After the rough shape is defined begin the actual carving. First isolate the nose, keeping the cheek line in mind. The line from the nostril to the corner of the mouth is important because it controls the face's expression. The line under the eye is another key expression line.

Wood carving can be useful for small (12″ to 18″—i.e., 30.5 cm to 45.7 cm) puppets. However, it has fallen into disuse with larger puppets, since the wood tends to make puppets too heavy. Wood carving is an art in itself, and a practitioner could easily devote a lifetime to it.

Clay, soap, and other materials used in modeling and carving are often too heavy to be used in a finished puppet. To reproduce a clay figure for puppetry, you need to make a mold. Then you may cast any lighter material (such as liquid latex or Styrofoam) in or around the mold to make a figure that is suitable for a finished puppet.

There are at least two advantages to casting. First, you end up with a figure that is light enough to use in a puppet. And second, if the figure gets bumped around too much, you can always cast another just like it from the permanent mold.

Making Casts

In this chapter we will learn two methods of casting. In "positive casting" a piece of a puppet is made by shaping puppet materials *over* a mold. The positive mold is smaller than the desired finished product, and need not be intricately detailed. Detail is given to the outer, sculpted cast piece, the puppet piece itself.

In "negative casting" a mold is made over a model and the puppet materials are cast *inside* the mold. The fine details of the (usually) clay model are faithfully picked up by the mold, and accurately reproduced in the finished cast piece.

Because casting materials sometimes stick to the mold, a mold release substance may be required. The following chart outlines releases which are effective with casting materials.

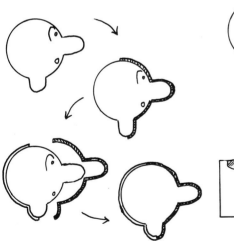

Positive mold process: Make a sculpture. Cover it with the right mold release and the casting material. Remove the cast shell and glue the cast pieces together.

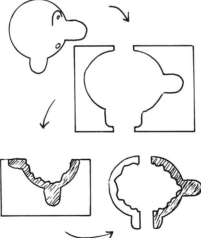

Negative mold process: Make a sculpture. Make a mold around the sculpture. Put casting material *inside* the mold. Remove the cast and glue the pieces together.

Molds and Casting

A Guide to Casting

Original Sculpture	Mold Material	Mold Release	Casting Material	Recommended Skill Level
Positive Molds:				
The mold is the original sculpture.	Clay	None	Papier-mâché	Beginner
	Balloons	None	Papier-mâché	Beginner
	Chicken Wire	None	Papier-mâché	Beginner
	Chicken Wire	Leave wire in	Cloth Mâché	Intermediate
	Potatoes	None	Papier-mâché	Beginner
	Wood	Aluminum Foil	Papier-mâché	Intermediate
	Wood	Aluminum Foil	Cloth Mâché	Intermediate
	Wood	Aluminum Foil	Celastic	Advanced
	Tissue Mâché	Aluminum Foil or destroy mold	Celastic	Advanced
Negative Molds:				
Clay original, finely detailed.	Plaster	Shellac/Wax	Papier-mâché	Intermediate
	Plaster	Water	Plastic Wood	Intermediate
	Plaster	None	Liquid Latex	Advanced
	Plaster	Shellac/Wax	RTV Silicone	Very Advanced
	Latex	None	Fiberglass	Very Advanced
	Latex	None	RTV Silicone	Very Advanced
	RTV Silicone	None	Fiberglass	Very Advanced

Some of the materials listed above may pose health hazards. Please read carefully the sections on the methods you use and follow safety recommendations.

A positive mold is an object that can be covered with a cast, much as a broken arm is covered with a plaster cast. The cast in puppetry, however, is cut off and used in a show.

Positive molds can be made of such materials as clay, balloons, chicken wire, potatoes (and some other vegetables and fruits), wood, and any other substance that can be shaped through carving, modeling, or carpentry.

Clay

You can make just about anything out of clay by modeling, pinching, braiding, coiling, and smoothing. Clay has two undesirable qualities for use in puppetry, however. It is heavy and it is too easily reshaped, being soft. If you want to make a witch's head you may start with clay, but you can't use clay as the finished puppet. You can, however, cover the clay with a skin made of papier-mâché. When it has dried, the papier-mâché skin (or cast) may be removed from the clay head (positive mold) and reassembled, producing a papier-mâché head without the clay inside. The witch's head thus may be made of a more durable substance than clay and is light enough to be used in puppetry.

Balloons

Balloons can be molded and twisted and shaped into many forms that may become useful puppets or puppet parts. They are too light for puppetry, though, and pop easily. A balloon can be covered with a more durable skin, such as papier-mâché, to give it greater endurance on a puppet stage. To make a puppet head over a round balloon, you can add features by sculpting further with papier-mâché or by painting them on. It is easy to remove the positive mold (balloon) from inside the finished head (papier-mâché cast) by popping the balloon and pulling it out. Because this mold is so light, you could as well leave the balloon inside the cast.

Chicken Wire

Chicken wire, hardware cloth, or metal screening may be used to make a positive mold. It is about as simple as beginning sewing. You can shape chicken wire by snipping with tin snips, bending the wires together, pushing and pulling and forming. Cloth mâché and tissue mâché (explained later in this chapter) are good casting materials to use on chicken wire. Some casts on chicken wire require that the wire mold be left inside; other casts may be cut off the mold and reassembled.

Potatoes

Potatoes and some other vegetables and fruits can be carved or used just as they are for positive mold shapes. Papier-mâché and Celastic are good casting materials to use on these positive molds. The cast form will look much like the potato, carved potato, or whatever the original mold was.

Wood

Some puppet companies make a standard sized puppet body out of wood as a positive mold for all their puppet bodies. Wood must be covered with aluminum foil before casting is done. Papier-mâché, cloth mâché, and Celastic are good casting materials to use on wood.

Casting on Positive Molds

A positive cast is the hollow replica of an original smaller carved or modeled figure. Since a positive cast is taken from around a figure, it only reproduces the broadest details. You must therefore exaggerate features such as noses, chins and brows in the original figure (the model) to assure that they will appear in the final cast figure. For this reason, limit the use of positive casting to large objects from materials such as clay, balloons, wire forms, and carved potatoes where details are not vital.

Casting Papier-mâché

To make the shape of a body or head, use a balloon for a mold under a papier-mâché cast. Should the balloon deflate after it is covered with papier-mâché, blow another one up *inside* the cast. The cast can usually be saved. Once the cast is dry, pop the balloon and remove it.

A papier-mâché cast on a block of carved wood requires a mold release, otherwise the glue in the papier-mâché will stick to the wood. Cover the wood mold with aluminum foil before applying the glued

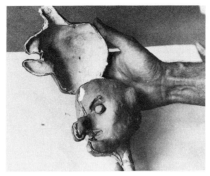

paper. This should also be done before applying glue-soaked cloth.

Modeling clay can be covered by papier-mâché, too. Cover the figure and let dry. Either cut a seam all the way around the cast and remove the mold (as shown here), or cut a small hole in the cast and scoop out the mold with a spoon.

Apply a white glue to the cut edges of the cast after the mold has been removed. Squeeze the two halves of the cast together, making the seam as inconspicuous as possible. Tape the two halves together until the glue dries. Then apply small pieces of laminated papier-mâché over the seam to strengthen and hide it.

Casting Celastic

Celastic goes on like papier-mâché and endures like wood. It is the mainstay of the professional puppet maker. It is a tough, waterproof, cellulose-impregnated fabric that becomes self-adhesive when immersed in a solvent such as acetone, methyl ethyl ketone (MEK), or methyl acetate. Celastic may be purchased at theatrical supply houses and major art supply houses. It works well on positive molds and in negative molds.

Wear rubber gloves to protect your hands; some plastic gloves dissolve in solvent. These solvents also give off toxic vapors and are highly combustible. Use them only in a well-ventilated room. The glue can be removed with a solvent-soaked cloth.

Prepare mold by covering it with aluminum foil; this will be the mold release. Tear, do not cut, squares and strips of Celastic (to insure a smoother finish, feather the edges).

After soaking Celastic in solvent for a few seconds, it will become soft and malleable as wet fabric. At this stage, the Celastic may be used as a cast. Apply the squares and strips to the mold like laminated papier-mâché.

Celastic casting (positive casts).

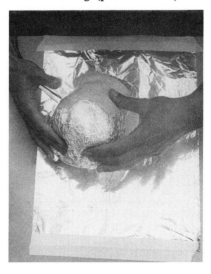

Positive Casts

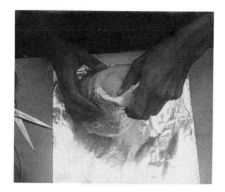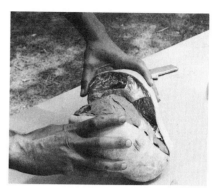

Celastic casting

Within three minutes, as the solvent evaporates, Celastic takes on the rigidity of soft leather and is no longer self-adhesive. It can be draped, formed, and sculpted at this stage and is good for making trees, castles and other parts of scenery. After thirty to sixty minutes, the solvent-soaked Celastic takes on an almost stonelike hardness and permanently holds its shape. When Celastic is dry, cut a seam all around the cast with a mat knife. Remove the mold (and aluminum foil release) from cast. (A sculpted, chicken wire mold can be left inside a Celastic cast. A tissue mâché mold will be destroyed as it is ripped out.) Tack the halves of the cast back together with masking tape. Cover the seam with more Celastic.

Wet Celastic will adhere to dry Celastic. A Celastic surface can be sanded, repaired and painted.

Making Negative Molds

Any material that can pour and then solidify can be used to make a negative mold. Plaster of paris is the most natural choice for such purposes. It creates a rigid mold that picks up details exactly. Molds may also be formed with less traditional media, such as liquid latex. Liquid latex and RTV (room-temperature-vulcanized) silicone result in flexible molds.

After preparing either rigid or flexible molds, allow them to set for about thirty minutes, then pry figure halves out of the molds. Theoretically, the mold halves will pop apart and the figure can easily be removed. If you have difficulty, however, make certain that you do not mar the imprint made in the plaster, thus ruining a mold. Although it is desirable, the figure itself does not have to be preserved. If a mold does break, it can usually be glued back together with little or no harm done to the imprint. Once the mold is pried apart, wash it before using.

Rigid Molds

Rigid molds are most often made from plaster of paris. An inexpensive medium derived from powdered gypsum, it has been in use for over 5000 years. When dry, plaster of paris acts like a rigid sponge, sucking moisture away from the material in the mold and passing it through the absorbent plaster to the air, where it is evaporated. Pay attention to detail when mixing plaster of paris to avoid pinholes and bubbles and to insure an even distribution of moisture throughout the mold.

Plaster hardens because of a chemical reaction, not because the water in the mixture evaporates. This chemical reaction can be set off by heat, both from hands or hot water, agitation, or contact with already mixed or hardened plaster. For this reason, keep the work area, your tools, and your hands as clean as possible.

Because plaster will not produce noxious fumes, all you need is a clean, comfortable work area with a table and a nearby source of water. The powder is fine and gets into everything, so do not work in rooms with rugs.

Do not wash plaster off your hands into a sink with running water; it will collect in the water trap in the drain, harden, and permanently damage the pipes. To avoid this problem, install plaster traps, and empty when necessary, or use a disposable paper painter's bucket filled with water. Allow the plaster to settle and harden in the bucket, then simply toss in the garbage. It is also advised that young people work with plaster only under supervision. If swallowed, a rock of plaster could form in the stomach.

Preparing Plaster

Read the directions on the box. Since there are many different consistencies of plaster, from Casting Plaster to Hydro-Stone (hardest of all) directions vary from product to product. Do not use spackle or patching plaster because these contain lime. If you can, use plaster of paris (also called United States Gypsum's Moulding Plaster). Choose plaster of paris with a middle-grade hardness and setting time. Setting times vary according to room temperature; the best working temperatures are between 70° F and 80° F. Setting times also vary with agitation, the length of contact it has with hands, the relative humidity and other atmospheric conditions. Plaster is cheap, so if a batch goes hard too fast, start over with clean buckets and clean hands.

Fill mixing bucket to no more than one third with COLD water. (If possible, allow the water to stand for several hours to insure against air

Negative Molds

General procedures for using plaster of paris.

bubbles in the plaster mixture.) Sift two parts plaster powder to the one part of cold water, pouring slowly over your (dry) hand to break larger granules and lumps into fine powder before it hits the water.

When powder mounds up in the water to resemble a miniature volcanic cone the mix is approximately two to one. Allow to stand for four to five minutes to soak the powder and drive the air bubbles out. When the mixture settles, the water should just cover the powder. If there is too little plaster, add some more; if there is too much plaster, add water. This is the only time you can adjust the proportions.

When ready to work, stir or agitate the plaster-water mixture thoroughly, using your fingers or a mixing stick to break up the lumps. (The chemical reaction will not be set off without agitation, heat, or contamination.) When the plaster begins to have the consistency of cream, tamp bottom of the bucket to make any air bubbles rise out.

After the chemical reaction is set off, you have between seven and fifteen minutes to work with it, during which time it passes through three of its five consistencies. The first stage is like liquid cream and can easily be poured. The second stage is like whipped cream or frosting. For about a minute or two, it peaks like beaten egg whites and can be applied with a spatula. The consistency of the third stage is like cheese and is no longer good for applying as a mold. The fourth stage resembles soft soap stone (carvable but almost set) and the fifth is like a rock although not a very strong one (this occurs after approximately thirty minutes).

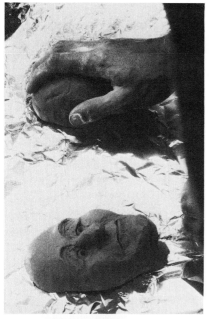
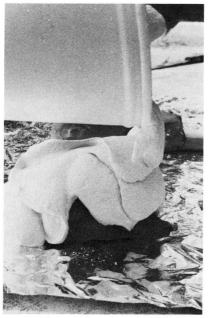

Simple halved mold, plaster of paris.

Simple Halved Mold

In this process and in the three following, a clay head is used for the original sculpture. For a simple halved mold, cut a clay puppet head into front and rear halves. Place halves, flat side down, on a sheet of aluminum foil far enough apart so the two will not touch.

Mix plaster, and when it is in the first, liquid-cream stage, pour a coating over both halves of the figure.

As the plaster moves into the second (or whipped-cream) stage pour or spatula enough over the first layer, which is still wet, to a thickness of 1″ (2.5 cm) or 1½″ (3.8 cm). Because plaster and clay don't stick to one another, no mold release is necessary.

This is a finished puppet that was made using a simple halved mold to form the head.

Allow to set for approximately thirty minutes. Pry figure halves out of the molds. The molds are ready for use after they are washed in soap and water.

Keyed Box Mold

First make a box. Because there is no real value in having a thick mold, do not make the box much larger than the object being molded. Use cardboard, or encircle the figure with a dike of modeling clay. The only requirement is that it not allow the plaster to seep through.

Remove the armature and sculpt a neck in its place. Suspend the object in the box to allow the plaster to flow around and under it. The simplest way to do this is to make a stand with three or four toothpicks. Simply push the toothpicks into inconspicuous parts of the figure.

Position the figure on these temporary legs in such a way as to minimize undercuts. A good example of an undercut is a hooked nose. If the nose hooks into the plaster, you will never get the mold off without breaking the nose. By tilting the head back, so the nose points up, an undercut is minimized.

Mix a small batch of plaster. While it is in the first, liquid-cream stage, pour it into the box up to, but not over, the halfway point on the figure so that when the plaster is dry you will be able to lift it out easily.

When the plaster goes into the second, whipped-cream stage, drop two or three marbles gently onto the surface of the plaster in various spots around the figure. Nudge the marble into the plaster to more than half the marble's diameter.

When the plaster is in the third, cheese-textured stage, remove the marbles so that hemispherical indentations are left. These will be the *keys* after which the mold is named. The next pouring of plaster will fill the marble holes, so the two plaster pieces of the finished mold may be alligned exactly when put back together for casting.

Allow the plaster to dry at least thirty minutes. Rub petroleum jelly over the top surface of the plaster, making certain the demispherical indentations left by the marbles are also coated. (Do not coat a Plasticene figure; it contains its own linseed oil, and an application of petroleum jelly would only blur the features of the figure.)

Mix more plaster, and when it is still in the liquid-cream stage, pour it over the figure and fill up the box to at least 1″ (2.5 cm) thickness over the highest point of the figure. Allow the second batch of plaster to dry thoroughly before prying the mold halves apart.

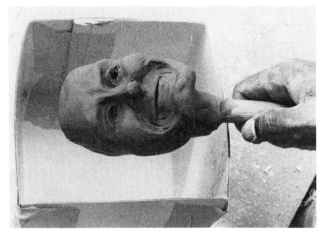

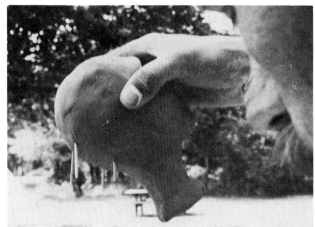

Box (or keyed) mold, plaster of paris.

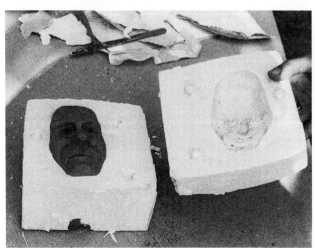

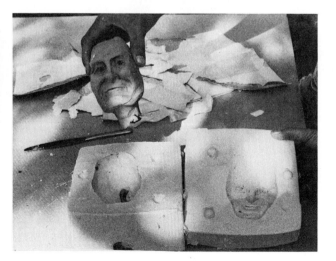

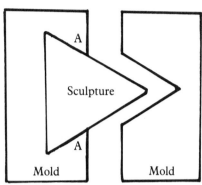

Theoretically, the mold halves should simply pop apart and the figure be easily removed. If you have difficulty, however, make certain you do not mar the imprint made in the plaster, thus ruining the mold. Although it is desirable, the figure itself does not have to be preserved. After the mold has been thoroughly washed with soap and water, it can be used to make a wood dough head such as the one used on this finished puppet.

An undercut mold cannot be removed from the sculpture. The sculpture is trapped in the left half of the mold at points "A" in this drawing, while the right half of this mold is removed easily.

A box mold was used to make this puppet.

Modified Margo Rose Mold

This is a three-part mold made with one mixing of plaster. In the previous three methods, the armature was removed and a sculpted neck was created. In this method, leave the armature in, and sculpt the neck around it.

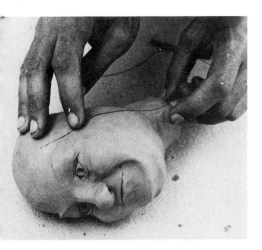

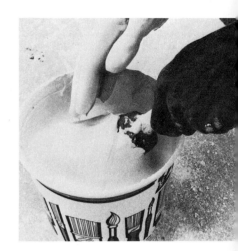

Starting at the base of the neck, gently embed a length of cobbler's thread vertically into the neck and up to the top of the head. Circle the crown of the head as though outlining a skull cap with the thread. (At one point, the thread will overlap itself.) Continue down the other side of the head to the bottom of the neck. Thread should extend well beyond the neck and armature at both ends.

Mix a sizable portion of plaster (enough to cover the entire figure). While it is still in the liquid-cream stage, either pour it over the face of the mold or dip whole head into the plaster. Make certain the entire figure is covered. And make certain you do not bump any part of the figure, especially its delicate features, against the side of the bucket.

As the plaster thickens into the second, whipped-cream stage, use a spatula or your hands to apply a layer to a thickness of about 1″ (2.5 cm). Smooth over the outside of the mold when the plaster reaches the third, soft-cheese stage.

Those who are experienced can do this next step with only one hand free, but most beginners will need both hands free. Quickly set the armature in a vice or have someone hold it. When the plaster goes into the third, cheeselike stage, *before it gets hard*, grab both ends of the cobbler's thread and unzip them, pulling carefully through the plaster to separate the three parts of the mold. This task must be accomplished before the plaster slips into the fourth, soft soap stone consistency, so it requires careful timing. If the plaster is too soft, the parts will ooze back together and the mold will not be usable. If the plaster is too hard, the cobbler's thread will not pull through it. Set aside to dry for at least thirty minutes.

No keys are needed, since the thread slices the plaster unevenly and the mold parts fit together like pieces of a puzzle. Wash thoroughly with soap and water, and the mold is ready for use.

Margo Rose mold.

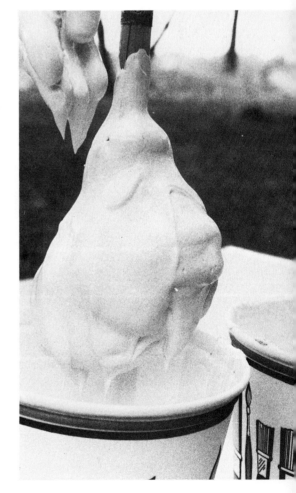

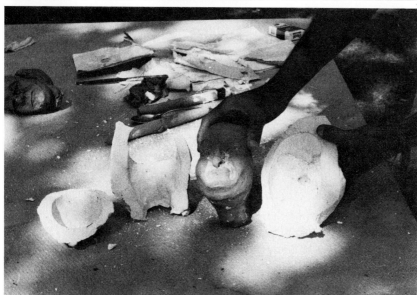

Shivs or Flanges

These, too, are irregularly edged molds that fit together like pieces in a puzzle. They require two mixings of plaster, but careful timing is not as crucial as it is with the modified Margo Rose mold.

Insert triangular flanges or shivs of metal into the side of the figure to be molded. (A lightweight aluminum will do, but not aluminum foil.) Place these flanges all around the figure in an uneven line, remembering to position the figure so as the minimize undercuts.

Mix plaster, and when it is still in the liquid-cream stage, pour a thin layer all over the front of the figure. When it is in the whipped-cream stage, apply another layer to the thickness of about 1″ (2.5 cm).

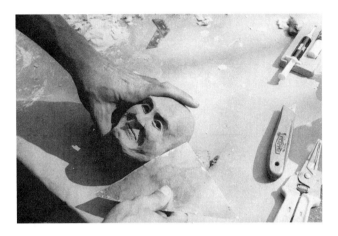

Shivs or flanges in mold-making
with plaster of paris.

After it has dried for at least thirty minutes, turn the figure over. Remove flanges, and apply petroleum jelly to the exposed edges of the plaster. With a second batch of plaster, apply two coats over the back of the figure as you did on the front half of the figure.

Set aside to dry for no less than thirty minutes. Pry apart mold halves and carefully remove the figure.

As can be seen in the above example of a flanged mold, the edges are uneven and fit together like pieces of a puzzle. The flanged or shiv mold does not require keys to make the two parts fit together properly.

Negative Molds

Flexible Molds

Liquid Latex Molds

With these kinds of molds, there is nothing to mix and there is plenty of working time (the length of time available before the product becomes too unmalleable to work). **To prevent inhalation of ammonia, always use liquid latex in well-ventilated areas.**

Pour a quantity of liquid latex into a container. The container need not be disposable. Since latex can be pulled off most surfaces after it dries, you can use your container more than once.

Mount (or leave) the figure on an armature. Pour liquid latex over the outer surface of the object. (The object may also be dipped, but dipping requires using more latex, and because the latex starts to cure, you have to pour the bowl of latex back into an airtight container between applications.)

Allow the first coat to set for twenty to thirty minutes. The rubber will change from a pale caucasian flesh color to amber as it cures. Do not wait for a full cure. Just when the first coat begins to darken slightly and while it is still tacky, apply a second coat. If you wait too long the layers will delaminate, rendering the mold useless. Repeat this process a third time.

While waiting for the third coat to get tacky, cut up squares of raw burlap. The size of the squares depends on the size of the figure being reproduced. Use burlap from gunny sacks, since the burlap from fabric stores is treated and not very absorbent. Dip the burlap into a bowl of liquid latex. Work the rubber into the fabric.

While the third coat is still tacky, laminate the entire exterior of the mold with the rubber-soaked burlap. The burlap acts as a filler and strengthens the mold, saving time and money.

The number of layers of burlap and rubber depends on the size of the object being molded. If your mold requires a thicker coat, wait until the first layer of laminations is partially cured, and using the same process described above, apply another layer of rubber-soaked burlap to the entire surface of the mold.

Set aside for four or five days, or in a low heat for several hours. Liquid latex cures, or vulcanizes, either with heat or time. Obviously, do not use heat to cure it if the original sculpture melts in heat (as does Plasticene).

When the latex feels as strong as a rubber band, cut the mold open with a mat knife. Remove the clay figure from the mold and put the mold in a low heat oven for several hours to complete the cure. Mold is then ready for use.

Negative Molds

Making a liquid latex mold.

67

Negative Molds

RTV Silicone Molds

RTV (room temperature vulcanized) silicone is not rubber, but a plastic that behaves like rubber. RTV silicone does not stick to anything when cured, and it cures at room temperature in much less time than liquid latex.

Different densities of RTV silicone are available. Some kinds are able to withstand temperatures high enough to be used in casting molten metals. This substance comes in two parts which have to be mixed. Generally it is more expensive than liquid latex. After mixing, RTV rubber has the consistency of a syrup and should be used in small box molds. When it cures, it will not stick to anything and faithfully reproduces details.

Casting in Negative Molds

Negative molds, such as those described in the preceding pages, are molds which enclose a space. The shape of your cast puppet pieces will be determined by the *inside* surface of the mold, if you use a negative mold. We will be using the molds formed in the preceding section for making some of these casts.

Casts in negative molds can be made from a variety of materials. **Some casting materials are more difficult and more dangerous to use than other materials. Always read the labels for full instruction and safety warnings when using any material.** Also check the chart for the compatibility of your desired casting material with the type of mold you have. Remember that unless you use a release, the mold and cast must be made of materials that won't stick together.

Casting Plastic Wood

In puppetry, the most commonly used material for negative casts is plastic wood, sometimes called wood dough.

You can make homemade plastic wood by mixing white glue and sawdust. This is tedious, messy, and the end product is not as uniformly good as commercially available wood dough. Homemade plastic wood, is, however, cheaper and safer.

Commercially prepared plastic wood is available in most hardware stores. A one-pound can is enough for the average puppet head. It tends to dry out quickly once a can is open, so buy only as much as you will use. An acetone solvent is available, also, to reconstitute partially dried plastic wood. **Caution is required (see below) when using commercial plastic wood. Homemade plastic wood is preferred when children will be involved.**

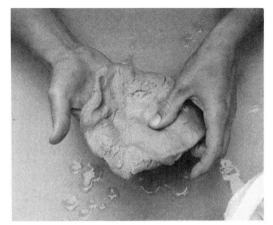
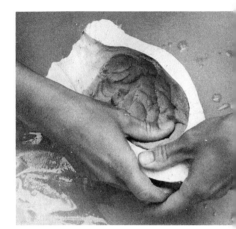

Casting plastic wood in simple halved and keyed molds.

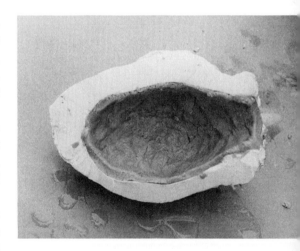

Plastic wood sticks to metals, wood, glass and stone. It is a malleable material that hardens through evaporation of its solvents to give a surface and body that can be sanded, cut, drilled, planed, whittled, stained, varnished, painted or lacquered, that will hold screws or nails and otherwise behave like wood. Always work with wet hands or it will stick to you, too.

Commercial plastic wood is extremely flammable. Its vapors should not be breathed, and it should not be swallowed because it contains toluene and aliphatic ketones as a solvent. Always work in a ventilated area and keep this product out of reach of children. If young people use it, they should be under proper supervision.

To work with plastic wood in a plaster cast, place both halves of a mold in a bucket of water for no less than fifteen minutes. While plastic wood adheres to dry plaster, it does not adhere to water-soaked plaster. Keep your hands wet when working with wood dough, otherwise the plastic wood will stick to you.

Make a thin (about ⅛" or .3 cm thick) pancake of plastic wood about 2" (5.0 cm) in diameter. Place the flattened plastic wood over the mold cavity and gently press it into the mold, making sure it is pushed into all the finest details of the mold. Should a small hole appear, simply patch it with a small lump of plastic wood. Work slowly. Make certain the edges of the cast are thick, since they will be joined to the other half.

Make another pancake of plastic wood and repeat the procedure for the other half of the mold.

Negative Casts

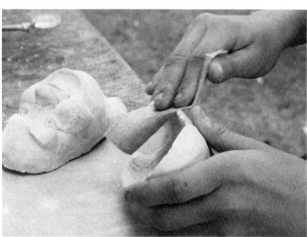

Place both halves of the mold, plastic wood and all, into a bucket of clean water. (Plastic wood "dries" under water.) Keep the halves submerged overnight.

Because plastic wood tends to shrink as it dries, it is usually easy to remove from a cast. If a nose or some other small part breaks off, just glue it back in place with white or carpenter's glue. Place a piece of sandpaper on a table and sand the edges of the front and back halves until they are flat. The edges distort a little, so a touch-up sanding might also be necessary to make certain the outside edges of the cast halves are the same.

Place a bead of glue all around the edge of one of the cast halves, then glue the halves together. Wrap gaffer's tape around the cast to act as a clamp while it dries. Once the glue dries, the solid, three-dimensional casting can be used as, in this case, a finished puppet head.

Casting Liquid Latex in Keyed Molds

Remember to work in well-ventilated areas when using liquid latex. A hollow, all-rubber cast is easy. Put the two parts of a keyed mold together and wrap with gaffer's tape. Pour in liquid latex and let stand overnight. The longer the mold stands, the thicker the cast becomes. Acrylic paint can be used to color uncured latex.

As the solvent dissipates, you may have to refill the mold slightly. Solvent dissolves outward, through hardening rubber and plaster, so rubber skin forms where you want it. Anywhere from a half to one day setting time will give a durable, hollow, rubber cast. Pour excess liquid latex back into can. Place mold, with cast still inside, in a low heat oven for several hours. Remove the cast, and with scissors remove the flange film formed by the seam. Cast is ready for painting.

Realistic hands can also be made in a keyed mold with liquid latex, but the procedure is slightly different. Have liquid latex, wire, and cotton batting on hand and prepare to work in a well-ventilated area.

Using the molds as models, make armatures of wire to simulate the fingers and the hand itself. Extend a loop of wire out beyond each mold; this will serve to connect the hands and the wrists.

Remove the wire armatures and paint the inside of both halves of the mold with a thin layer, or gel coat, of liquid latex. (Do not use a good paintbrush since it will be ruined once the latex cures.) When the gel coat begins to darken and become tacky in about twenty to thirty minutes, add another coat. Repeat for three or four coats.

Casting liquid latex in a keyed mold.

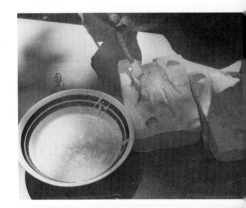

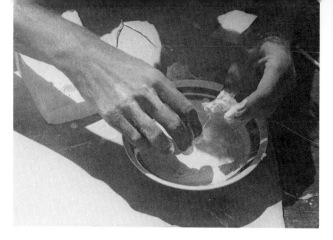

While waiting between coats, separate small tufts from a roll of cotton batting, and dip them into a bowl of latex. Work latex into cotton. (Do not use polyester "cotton" because it does not absorb well.)

Roll the tufts and place one in each finger of the molds. Place a wad of latex-soaked cotton in the palm areas as well. Lay the wire armatures in place on bottom halves of the molds. Press top and bottom halves of molds together, and tape tightly with gaffer's tape. Set in a low heat oven for several hours.

When you remove rubber cast of hand from mold, you can bend fingers and shape the hand to any desired expression. Then the cast can be finished with a coat of paint.

Casting Liquid Latex in Large Molds

Working in a well-ventilated area, begin a large rubber cast, the same as above, by painting a gel coat on the inside of the mold halves (four to six coats).

Cut up pieces of untreated burlap to be used as filler-binder. Saturate the pieces of burlap with latex and apply to gel coat while it is still tacky. Cover both halves of the mold thoroughly, making sure to overlap the burlap squares. Then paint a heavy application of latex around the edges of the mold. Put both halves of the mold together, taping or tying them in place. Cure in a low heat oven for several hours.

When you separate the halves, you will have a flexible rubber casting that can be painted (with flexible latex paint), and decorated. These are Morlocks from the Bennington Puppets' production of *The Time Machine*.

NOTE: The excess rubber drippings on glass or plastic bowls can leave quite a mess to clean up. Instead of cleaning up right away, let the latex cure for a day or so. Then it will be a snap to pull off the latex.

 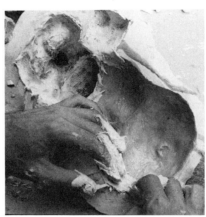 

Casting liquid latex in large molds.

Casting Fiberglass in a Latex Mold

When working with fiberglass (actually fiberglass impregnated with polyester resin), work in a well-ventilated room, away from heat, sparks, and open flames. Avoid prolonged breathing of its vapors. Polyester resin can be bought in quantity from wholesalers and sculpture supply houses, or from hardware stores and auto shops as auto repair kits.

The polyester resin comes in two components: a filler and a hardener. With a clean mixing stick, stir the filler before using (the ingredients sometimes separate). Scoop out enough to make a 4″ (10.2 cm) pancake about ¼″ (.6 cm) thick on a sheet of aluminum foil taped to a table. Polyester resin sticks to everything and becomes as hard as metal, so do not work directly on tables or counters.

Squeeze the hardener out of its tube, laying a 2″ (5.0 cm) ribbon across the pancake. The fiberglass repair kits available at most hardware stores come with a booklet in full color showing the grey pancake and the red hardener mixing to the proper dirty pink. Match this color. If it is too red, it becomes hard too fast. If it is too grey, it may never really harden.

Simply apply the resin to the inside of the latex mold (no release is necessary). As much as possible, turn the latex mold inside out. Use a tongue depresser, ice cream stick or knife you won't need anymore. Apply a net to the inside of the first layer of polyester resin in the mold. (Most auto repair kits come with a plastic mesh for a filler-binder.) Do not make a solid casting: it will be too heavy and too expensive. The mesh will hold the polyester resin in place in the mold.

Negative Casts

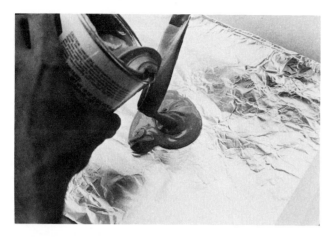

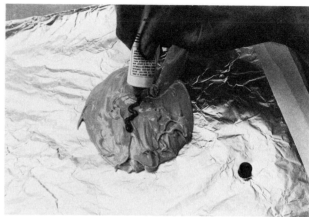

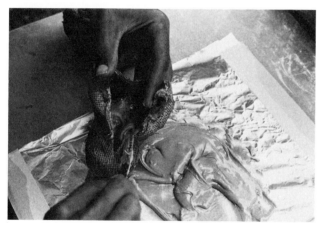

Casting fiberglass.

When the resin embedded with plastic mesh is about ⅛″ (.3 cm) thick, turn the latex mold right side in. Within thirty minutes, depending on mixture, humidity and heat, the resin will harden. Remove from latex mold. The casting is still sandable for from four to six hours. After that, it becomes almost indestructable.

3

SHADOW PUPPETS

A shadow puppet may include great detail, as does this Indonesian rawhide puppet.

Backstage during *Tyl Eulenspiegel's Merry Pranks*, produced by The Underground Railway Puppets and Actors. The puppeteer wears a harness to support the weight of the clear lexan plastic puppet. The puppeteer's hands thus are free to manipulate the hands and feet of the puppet in this shadow show. See the back cover for an example of the bright color in these puppets. Photograph by Lista Duren.

Shadow puppets are two-dimensional figures, manipulated behind a translucent screen through which they are viewed as shadows. Alternatively, they can be transparencies, with articulated parts, manipulated on an overhead projector. In a way, animated cartoons are really shadow puppets.

Legend has it that an enterprising Chinese man named Chiao-meng created an elaborate silhouette of the Emperor's deceased wife in 120 B.C. He projected it on a back-lighted cotton screen and told the mourning Emperor that it was the spirit of the departed Empress. When the Emperor discovered the hoax, after taking a good deal of advice from his "wife" on matters of state, he had Chiao-meng executed. But, in China, Chiao-meng achieved immortality as the inventor of shadow puppetry, and the screen is still called the *screen of death*.

Shadow puppets are just shadows of any recognizable two-dimensional object. The four essential elements of shadow puppetry are the figures themselves, the control, the screen, and the light.

Making Shadow Puppets

Activated by a string, a simple Jumping Jack figure can become a lively shadow puppet.

Close-up of a shadow puppet from *Tyl Eulenspiegel's Merry Pranks*, produced by The Underground Railway Puppets and Actors. Photograph by Suzanne Marshall.

Shadow puppets can derive from many sources and perform in a variety of situations. Consult any number of the books that abound on folk art and traditional Chinese, Javanese, and Indian shadow puppets. Pictographs and cave paintings, embroideries and tapestries from many cultures and time periods will yield interesting ideas to animate as shadow puppets. Copy cartoon figures and have them perform in front of a landscape painting. The figure can bring the landscape to life and explain the painting for an art class. Figures can also be cut off magazine covers and perform in front of a picture of the world to discuss international affairs. Advertising art is loaded with possibilities. Use a puppet to explain how to shop wisely.

Shadow puppetry is usually a function of drawing, and children instinctively draw in a way that is very applicable to shadow puppetry.

Any two-dimensional piece of art can come to life. If you want to work in the traditional medium, use rawhide to duplicate sketched figures. However, since rawhide is hard to come by, try working with simpler materials. Start by drawing a figure on regular paper, and cut it out. To make a Jumping Jack figure, cut off the arms or legs that you want to move. Cement the dismembered figure to cardboard. When cutting out the cardboard, leave some extra at the top of the arms (or any joint) so that they will not be too short when they are joined to the shoulder. If you decide to make a cardboard puppet, allow for the overlap needed at the joints *before* cutting the figure out. Punch a hole in the shoulder and in the extra cardboard tab at the top of the arm. Fasten the joint together with a paper fastener or knotted string. If you make large figures out of cardboard, you might need to reinforce them with strips of wood glued to the back. Cut full-sized silhouettes of people out of stiff cardboard. Hinge the jaw for a talking puppet.

When making shadow puppets of people and animals, study their movement. Decide which movements are important or characteristic of your puppet, and capture the essence of those movements. Above all, keep it simple. Try, for instance, to avoid making extra joints in an animal's back. You will need none in most horses, one in most rabbits, probably two in a cat or tiger and a lot for most serpents. Use newspapers for your rough sketches. Experiment by cutting joints in different places. Once you have decided where they must go, transfer the idea to a stiffer medium.

Translating a full-color, three-dimensional, living figure into two dimensions may be difficult, but turning it into a shadow is a bigger challenge. The trick is to determine what a recognizable shadow is. The front view of a head is not as recognizable as a profile. Yet the eye is more easily recognizable from the front than it is in profile.

This rendition of a traditional Chinese tiger shows that the body is made with a joint at mid-body and at the neck. This is an "exploded" tiger that would be joined together with the wagon-wheel joints in the body and at the top of the four legs hidden behind the solid portions of the torso.

Five ovals, a curlicue and a stylized face with teeth and other features cut in make a fine recognizable dragon.

To indicate the kind of costume your shadow puppet is wearing, perforate it. Simply cut dotted lines into the puppet body to indicate the shape of a coat, the thickness of a belt, or the flashy exaggeration of a neck tie.

You can also make distinctive puppets by giving them some color. A common misconception about shadows is that they are just silhouettes. Although you can make puppets by simply cutting silhouettes of people from black paper, shadow puppets can actually appear in color on the screen if they are highly colored and translucent. In traditional rawhide puppets translucence was achieved by painting the puppets on both sides and saturating them in oil so that light could pass through them and through the applied colors. To achieve this effect with your puppet, paint it on thick, white paper and saturate it with alcohol or spray acrylic, **using safety procedures to protect eyes and lungs.** A safer method for making colorful shadows

The Turkish character Karaghioz, with face in profile, eye seen as in a front view.

Making Shadow Puppets

◀ Indonesian shadow puppets are usually made of rawhide, and details of dress and features are painted on, often in rich colors.

▶ In Turkish shadow puppetry, Beberuhi, the midget, demonstrates that details of dress can be cut into the shadow puppet. Because he was always in search of truth, a lantern, with its light shining through the shadows, can be seen dangling from the tip of his long hat. Notice that Beberuhi is created with a side-view face and a front-view eye, as is Karaghioz.

This young man from the Szechwan Province of China shows the spoked-wheel joints.

is to cut holes in the opaque material and glue colored tissue paper, cellophane or acetates over the holes. Transparent dyes on white drawing paper will also allow the color to show through the shadows. Plastics and colored inks also give bright, solid colors for puppets that will look like animated stained glass.

Tissue paper comes in a wide variety of colors. Mix the colors by overlapping the paper. Glue tissue to acetate or use thick sheets of colored acetate. You can also press autumn leaves, reeds, and grasses between sheets of waxed paper (with an iron) and arrange them to resemble fish, sunbursts, leaves or abstract designs. Because the waxed paper is not stiff, it must be stapled to a cardboard frame if you want to hold it up on controls.

Overlapping colors at the joints of a puppet become darker due to increased color density. To alleviate this problem, the Chinese developed a four-spoked wheel at the joints. By having the space between the spokes cut out, the figure retains its rigidity at the joint while being lighter, and it keeps the color density more uniform. The Chinese also put a smaller piece of leather between the overlapping joints to act as a "washer."

Scenery for shadow shows is sometimes hung directly against the screen to make the shadows distinct. Interesting effects can be created by paying attention to the laws of perspective that pertain to two-dimensional art, or by violating those laws cleverly.

Backstage, the Underground Railway puppeteers control Ivan, the boy hero, and a demon, in a scene from *The Firebird*, which was co-commissioned by the Boston Symphony, the Junior Committee of the Cleveland Orchestra, and Adventures in Music.

Out front, the brilliantly colored shadow puppets engage in conflict, eventually won by the boy's peaceful spirit and the magic of the golden Firebird. The demon becomes larger and more diffuse as the puppeteer backs it away from the screen.

The Control

The simplest way to control a shadow puppet is with a *vertical rod*. The rod can be made of anything that is straight and stiff, such as a dowel, umbrella spoke, stick, or wire. It must be big enough to support the figure, and may be taped, tacked, or sewn to the puppet. The rods used to manipulate arms, legs and other appendages may be smaller. Because the vertical rod is on the same plane as the figure, it is visible on the screen.

A less visible means of control is the *horizontal rod*. Lights may be placed, above, below or to the sides of the shadow screen. In a traditional Turkish arrangement, dowels 12″ to 18″ (30 cm to 45 cm) are attached to the figure perpendicular to its plane. This eliminates the shadow of the control from the screen.

There is also the *combination control* in which a rod is attached to the back of the figure, perpendicular to its plane, and is then bent down so the puppet can be controlled from below. The rod can be made of stiff, but bendable, wire. While this does not eliminate the shadow of the control in back-lighted shadow theaters, it does diminish its clarity and thus deemphasizes it.

If the control rod is to be sewn into your shadow puppet, it should have a hole through which to sew. Umbrella spokes are good for this purpose, or use a piece of wire bent to form a loop at the end. If you prefer to use a dowel as a control rod, drill a hole into it or tape a paper clip securely to the end. Dowels can also be tacked to the figure (add a

The Control

Vertical rods, with lights behind the screen, or horizontal rods, with lights below the screen may be used for shadow puppet control.

dollop of glue to be sure). For lighter puppets, try taping drinking straws to the backs of the figures.

To add handles to the bottom of the rod, wrap a piece of foam rubber around the rod. Or glue a wooden bead to the bottom, and insert it into a wooden dowel, a cork or piece of bamboo.

The Screen

The screen for shadow puppets can be made of various materials. Historically, it has been made of parchment in northern Africa, anything from paper to nettle fabric to fine silk in China, fine cotton cloth in Java, and ground glass in England and America. In every arrangement, the screen is translucent enough to register a shadow and the light strong enough to cast a shadow. You may use whatever materials are available to achieve this same effect.

For a simple, temporary screen, cut a piece of white paper or tracing paper to the size of the screen you want. Then glue it to a cardboard frame cut out in a single piece. While this type of screen is easy to make, it does not wear well.

To make a similar but more permanent screen, cut a frame out of chipboard, plywood, or Masonite. Do not make a frame out of flimsy wood: it might warp and twist unless you insert it into a solid stage. Miter the corners so that the joints are flat. Reinforce the corners with small, diagonal braces. Put these on the back of the frame so they cannot be seen from the front.

Stretch a sheet of clean, white cloth such as bleached muslin over the frame. Fasten it with tacks or with a staple gun. Instead of muslin

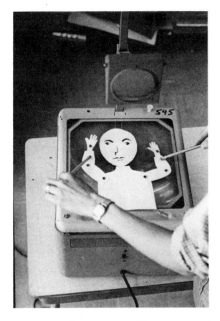

Shadow puppetry using an overhead projector.

you can also use poplin, cotton sheeting, nylon, rayon, or translucent acetates. You could also tack, pin, or staple a clean white sheet to a door frame, window frame, or artists' frame (for a painter's canvas, available in art supply stores).

Some puppeteers use screens as large as ten by twenty feet (3m × 6m). But the larger the screen, the more likely it is to sag and the more difficult to illuminate evenly. Screens up to two by five feet (.6 m × 1.5 m) will do for most projects. You can also use several small screens, side by side, to create a multistage theater. Store your screen in a plastic wrap: smudges show up markedly in shadow shows and are impossible to remove without taking the screen apart.

A sheet of ground glass makes a ready-made screen. You can even use a clear, glass window and let your puppets show their true colors.

The covered side of a screen can either face the audience (it looks neater) or the puppeteer. By facing the puppeteer, puppets can slide "off stage" rather than be picked off. When a shadow puppet is pulled back from the screen, it may grow bigger and its edges may blur, depending on the kind of light used. This can be very effective when it is done on purpose.

In place of a constructed screen, try using an overhead projector. The shadow figures are necessarily small, but they are easy to make. The "backstage" is the ground glass platform on the projector, while the "stage" is the wall, movie screen, or chalkboard upon which the figures are projected. For a variety of effects, use two or three overhead projectors. Put scenery on one and the actors on another.

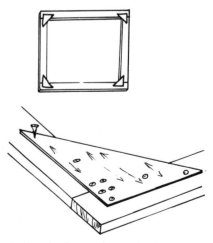

A simple frame for a shadow puppet screen can be made of 1 by 4 inch pine and quarter inch plywood.

The Screen

Put a scene change on a third, projecting all three in a kind of double exposure during scene changes. The puppeteer can actually be in the audience enjoying the show. You can use an overhead projector in combination with a more traditional backlit screen, as well.

Opaque projectors will not work; you cannot move the figures in the projecting tray when it is in place, and they get very hot quickly.

Most people think of a shadow screen as a profile of the real world where up is up and down is down and silhouettes saunter across with their feet firmly on the ground. But use your imagination. A screen can also be used as a floor plan, with the audience seeming to look down from above. Shadow puppets can easily defy gravity. They are also very good in wild fantasies.

The Light

The original light source for original shadow puppets was probably a campfire. Since then, torches, oil lamps, flashlights, the sun (hitting a cloth covered window), incandescent lights (single or in rows), spotlights and fluorescent light tubes have been used. Use an unfrosted incandescent bulb for a good light source. A floor lamp lighting a sheet stretched across a door frame works well.

A light situated behind the screen requires the puppeteers to hold their puppets up while they duck down (unless there is reason for the puppeteers' heads to appear in the show). In traditional Turkish shows, the lights are placed in a row right at the bottom of the screen to allow the puppeteer to stand up behind the screen, unseen, and gain better control of the puppets. Colored gels can be placed over lights for different moods.

Out Front

Although shadow puppets are traditionally shadows, there is no reason to confine this art to silhouettes. While Javanese women saw puppet shows through screens as shadows, Javanese men sat on the same side of those same screens as the puppeteers and saw the actual figures. Traditional Cambodian "shadow" puppets are manipulated in full view of the audience, in front of a 24'-wide (7.3 m) screen illuminated by an oil lamp. You can do the same! Any object drawn on a stiff piece of oaktag or non-corrugated cardboard and cut out can become a shadow puppet.

Shadow puppet plays are very suited to heightened forms of speech, such as song and poetry. Maybe because the visuals are so simple, they enable the audience to better appreciate the audio portions of such productions.

Many shadow puppets are easy puppets to make. They can be constructed out of easily worked material such as cardboard and oaktag. These simple puppets have a long tradition of performing wonderfully elaborate theatrical and educational tasks. Throughout the history of shadow puppetry, productions have proven to be simple enough that children can create and perform them. At the same time shadow shows are capable of a sophistication which keeps adult audiences interested.

In Java the traditional shadow puppets have traditional shapes for different characters. Heroes are forceful, have bulbous noses and rounded eyes, while this figure with his refined face and long sloping line from forehead to nose denotes a man of wisdom and distinction.

4

HAND PUPPETS

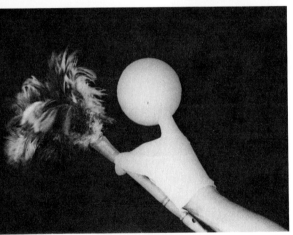

One characteristic of hand puppets is that they can manipulate other objects—a trait that makes it possible for Punch to punch and wreak havoc all over the set. No other type of puppet could achieve such mayhem.

The movement of a hand is the basis of all puppetry. Hand puppetry is the form most directly linked to the puppeteer.

The hand puppet's great advantage, besides simplicity of construction, is the immediacy of its control. Its great disadvantage is that the puppet is tied directly to the operator, and its breadth of movement is thus limited. Mouth puppets, finger puppets and body puppets all fall into this category. The control of hand puppets (called *glove puppets* in Britain) is immediate and direct. A puppeteer manipulates them from below by placing a hand inside the puppet body. This is probably the purest form of puppetry because the manipulator's personality (not the hand decoration) creates the puppet. Sergei Obrazov, the famed Russian puppeteer, has one sequence in which he uses bare hands topped by wooden balls for heads, minimally decorated. And a young West German puppeteer, using unadorned fingers, tells the tale of two worms getting to know one another.

If you want to go into great depth to learn to manipulate hand puppets, mime, the basis of all theatrical movement, is the best place to start. But it is enough for most puppeteers to muddle through and discover things on their own. Instinct is the best guide. A puppet that makes jerky motions with its head draws attention to itself as the one talking. Short, jerky movements can also connote happiness or surprise. Slow, cautious movement may connote fear, suspicion. And bouncing movement can connote running or dancing.

Practice in front of a mirror. One thing to watch for is eye contact. Be sure your puppet is "looking" at its audience by aiming its face at the proper angle. You do not want it looking off into the sky. Once this is mastered, the audience will be convinced the puppet is looking right at them.

When practicing with mouth puppets in front of a mirror, watch your own mouth movements and make your hand imitate them. There is a universal tendency to close your hands when the mouth should be open, and to open your hands when the mouth should be closed. It takes a little practice to reverse it.

Thumb and middle finger are easy to control. Thumb and little finger make more realistic arm motion.

There are many ways to hold the hand when controlling a hand puppet.

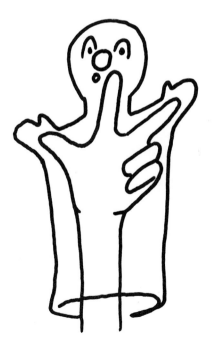

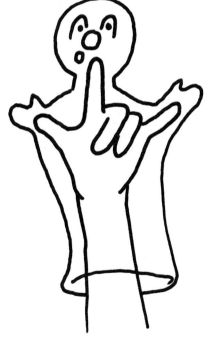

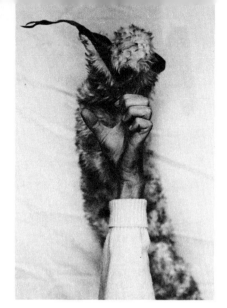

Practice with mouth puppets.

Making Hand Puppets

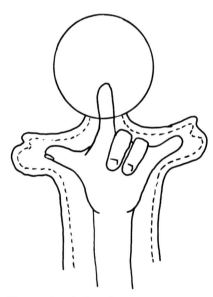

For a simple hand puppet pattern, trace around your hand and cut two pieces of fabric. Sew them together, and turn the unit inside out. Insert your hand and add a head.

The head of a human hand puppet is made essentially the same way as any puppet head, except that the bottom of the neck *must be open* to permit the fingers to enter. A hand puppet can be a simple mitten with "thumbs" on both sides. It can also be a glove, a sock, a cloth draped over a hand, or just a bare hand. Most mouth puppets are simply a little tube of cloth that fits over the hand and extends to cover the forearm. Many easy-to-make hand puppets are described in chapter one.

You can make a vicious, quilted shark by painting an evil eye on one side of an oven mitt. Add a fin to the heel of the mitt. Sew Styrofoam teeth to thumb and adjacent side. Insert hand, turning fingers sideways. Any mitten, used normally, with a face sewn, stapled, or painted to the palm, becomes a one-armed human or animal. If you do not need the mitten again, cut a hole in the thumbless side and add the other arm.

And what would we do without socks? Take a sock, and add a pair of plastic eyes. When placing hand inside, gather some cloth between fingers and thumb to make mouth (no cutting needed). Wrap a little feather boa around it, poke three pieces of thin wire into the tip of its nose, and you have a lion. Add felt ears and a crown made of twigs and you change it to a deer. A different set of ears plus a macrame rope bridle will look like a horse, especially if you use the feather boa as its mane (along length of arm). Or replace all this with a foam rubber shell and a "straw" hat-with-antennae and it is transformed into a

Although the easiest mouth puppets to make are dragons and snakes, mouth puppets can be full-sized people, such as these Tomten Puppets made by Karin Scott. A puppeteer manipulates the mouth and one arm of each puppet.

The Creation Production Company has a mouth puppet made of foam rubber. The puppeteer's hands operate the mouth, and one hand. Some puppets like this need another puppeteer to operate the other hand. Photograph by David Eisenreich.

snail. With contact cement, attach two foam-rubber discs (leaving two openings at opposite sides), cover with appropriate fabric with fringes for "legs" and slip your sock through to form a turtle. With the same sock, make a fist, gathering the cloth into the "mouth," add a miniature beret and you have a French artiste and a whole new line of almost-instant puppets.

Other kinds of puppets are possible when you *cut* a sock. If you slit the sock along the line of the foot and add a panel of cloth, a huge, expressive mouth emerges. This would be good for big-mouthed dragons, alligators, and even lions whose mouths must work overtime. For a mouth that snaps shut with a smug sound, glue a circle of cardboard, folded in half, to the tip of an inside-out sock. Turn sock right side in.

Cut a reversed sock down the middle of top and bottom of foot, almost to the heel. Sew the sides of cuts as though making a two-fingered glove. Turn sock right side in. Make a V with your hand and insert in sock with balled fist in the heel of the sock. With proper features added, it becomes a rabbit puppet with wiggly ears. On the back of the same sock, paint or sew on an upside-down human figure with feet at ear tips and head at about wrist level. Just by turning your bunny upside down and walking it on its ears, it magically becomes a little person.

Punch many tiny holes around the rim of a plastic funnel or the cut top of a detergent bottle. Sew the funnel to the end of a sock. Paint a face on the funnel for an anteater puppet.

A frequent mistake in hand puppetry is to make the body too short. If you intend to perform with a hand puppet, make sure the sleeve for the puppet body extends down to your elbow so that your arm or sleeve does not show.

Making Hand Puppets

On a thin arm, this sock becomes

a lion

or a deer

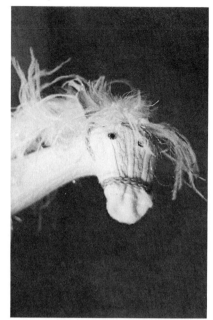

a horse

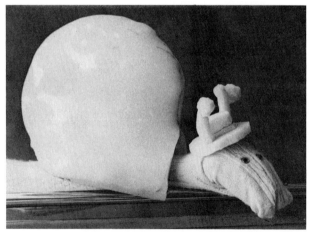

a snail

a turtle

a bunny

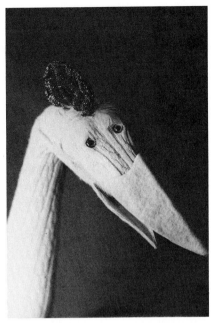

a bird, or

a French artiste.

 Bunched and tied at the toe, a sock can become many more puppet characters.

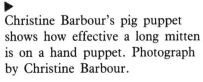 Christine Barbour's pig puppet shows how effective a long mitten is on a hand puppet. Photograph by Christine Barbour.

Of course, if you are going to make a fancy costume, such as the one seen on this ancient Chinese hand puppet, you will need a more elaborate pattern and imagination to match.

Sewing a puppet body is easy. First, make a pattern. Lay your hand on a sheet of newspaper, fingers spread in the way you intend to use them, and draw the outline, making the sleeve extend down to the elbow. Allow an extra inch or more width all around. Then cut out the pattern, and make the front and back in cloth. Sew up each side, leaving a hole for the head at the top and another for your arm at the bottom. If you plan to have hands on your puppet, leave a hole unsewn at the end of each arm. Finally, turn inside out (seams in), and attach the head and hands.

Anything into which you can cut or drill a hole for your finger can be made into a head. Tennis balls, rubber balls, wooden balls, may be left blank or decorated to resemble faces. Put one or two expressions on the same head for different dramatic moments for the same character. Heads do not have to be round, either. Styrofoam hamburger boxes make believable heads. Or cut an eight-ounce milk carton in the top peak to make the profile of a face. The simplest hands for these puppets are miniature mittens, made of cloth or felt of

Sew legs onto the body of the hand puppet. Usually these just hang and are manipulated by the quick movement of the wrist that makes them move as seen in this illustration. Some are made so fingers can go into the legs and manipulate them.

Two faces on one puppet.

any color. Trace a pattern on the cloth four times. Sew together in twos, leaving wrists open so your fingers can be inserted. Attach a collar or extension for more support and control. You can also stuff the mittens with cotton batting and close them off. These can be used on hand puppets, rod puppets and marionettes. More realistic hands can be modeled in clay and cast in plastic wood or liquid latex (see chapter 2).

For certain effects, sew legs onto the body of the hand puppet. Usually these just hang and are manipulated by the quick movement of the wrist that makes them seem to move. Puppet legs may be left

The Gingerbread Players combine puppets with people in a mobile, outdoor production. Photograph courtesy of Gingerbread Players.

Below left:
The mouse king holds the nutcracker in the Magic Puppet Theatre's production of *The Nutcracker Fantasy*. Photograph by Adelaide Ortegel.

Below right:
Pixie from *The Loch Ness Monster*, a puppet musical by Penny Jones and Company Puppets. Photograph by Shih-Tsung Chang.

An elephant by the Bennington Puppets with Marion Appel's giraffe and Jill Andersen Fortney's alligator demonstrate string, rod, and hand puppet designs on one stage.

One of Terry Rooney's Back Alley Puppets. Photograph by Patrick Cardin.

Foam rubber, styrofoam, fabric, and fur constitute these puppets created by Bonnie McCrea. Photograph by Karen Durlach.

From *The Cat Who Walked by Himself*, produced by Tidewater Traveling Puppet Theatre. Puppets by Judy Price and R. Eve Solomon. Photograph by R. Eve Solomon.

Gulliver's Travels puppets, made of cardboard and canvas painted and stuffed with wool. By Tidewater Traveling Puppet Theatre. Photograph by R. Eve Solomon.

Cloth and foam puppets from Tidewater Traveling Puppet Theatre's production of *Candide*. Photograph by R. Eve Solomon.

Bunraku puppets from Stravinski's *History of a Soldier*, performed by students at Saint Ann's School in Brooklyn, N.Y.

Larger than life-size puppet from the Underground Railway Puppets and Actors' production of Bertolt Brecht's *The Caucasian Chalk Circle*. Two actors manipulated each puppet, sometimes working in unison and sometimes playing different parts of the character's personality. Photograph by Chris Thomas.

Above left:
Olive the Octopus, created by Rachael Jennifer
Krygier.

Above right:
Morlocks, Dr. Watson, Inspector Lastrade, and
dinosaur from The Bennington Puppets' production
of H.G. Wells' *The Time Machine.*

Characters from Shakespeare's *Twelfth Night*,
produced by the Bennington Puppets.

Puppets reacting. Created by Terry Rooney for Back Alley Puppets. Photograph by Satoshi Kushiyama.

Hand puppet in action, by Terry Rooney for Back Alley Puppets. Photograph by Satoshi Kushiyama.

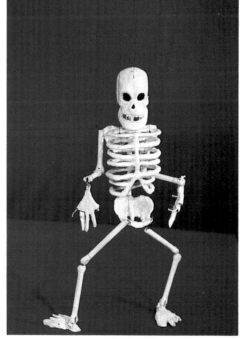

Right:
This marionette, Basil Rathbone, demonstrates great versatility in action. Created by The Bennington Puppets.

Left:
Thief from The Bennington Puppets'
production of *The Thief of Baghdad*.

Right:
One of Rochelle Lum's rod puppets
for Hinds' Feet puppet company.
Photograph by Michael Jang.

Puppetry in process. Puppet created
by Jan M. VanSchuyver for Dragon's
Wagon Theatre. Photograph by Molly
E. McDermott.

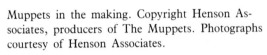

Muppets in the making. Copyright Henson Associates, producers of The Muppets. Photographs courtesy of Henson Associates.

Making Hand Puppets

More realistic heads can be modeled out of clay and cast in plastic wood (or liquid latex), such as these from the J M J Puppets.

empty or may be filled with cotton or polyester batting, crushed nut shells, or some other filler. Another alternative is to fill part of the leg and leave the top part open in order to insert the index and middle fingers of your other hand. Then you can make the puppet walk, dance or kick.

The most famous body puppet is a two-body puppet of a circus horse with one person in front for a head and front legs, and a second person in back for the tail and rear legs. Many two-hand puppets have a similar division of labor. One hand operates the neck and mouth of a goose, for example, and another hand wiggles its tail. Or one hand operates the lowing cow, and the other hand manipulates the tail in its battle against flies. You will often need a small armature or backbone in these two-hand puppets.

Two-hand Puppets

Cloth and foam were used in this princess and dragon, made by John McDonough for Pumpernickel Puppet Theatre. Photograph by Graphics East, Inc.

This stick puppet is part of the Children's Museum of the Native American in New York City.

This rod puppet from Rod Young's Creative Puppetry may be moved in a greater variety of ways than is possible with a stick puppet. Photograph by Westchester County, N.Y., Department of Parks and Recreation.

5

ROD PUPPETS

Rod puppets are manipulated from below or behind with sticks, rods or wires. This way the control is one step removed from the puppet itself. The major characteristic of rod puppets is gesture. Since they are mechanical puppets, subtlety of movement depends as much on the ingenuity of the builder as it does on the sensitivity of the manipulator. Rod puppets can be as simple as a paper plate attached to a stick (see chapter one), or as complex as a Japanese Bunraku puppet that requires three puppeteers to operate.

One advantage of rod puppets is that they can be held away from the puppeteer, yet, because the rods are stiff, control is direct and precise. Another advantage is that they have "backbones" and can be set in a play board or holding rail while the puppeteer manipulates their parts or other puppets. A major disadvantage of these puppets is that the rod is obviously visible whereas a marionette's strings almost always seem to disappear during a performance. Rods may be hidden in long sleeves or disguised as a walking stick or a broom.

The difference between rod and stick puppets is in the complexity of the controls. The stick puppet is a figure attached to *one* rod. A rod puppet usually involves additional rods and more complex inner controls for moving arms, legs and sometimes mouth and eyes.

The control is the heart of the rod puppet. In most puppets, it is a thick dowel which goes to the neck, used in conjunction with smaller rods to the hands.

A simple control rod is a dowel, passed through a vertical hole in the body and attached to the head. The Javanese Wayang Golek are usually built this way. A dowel permits the head to turn from side to side without moving the body. The rod usually has a collar to keep the head at the right distance from the shoulders. Of course, a trick puppet with a growing neck would need an extra long control rod which would allow the head to rise. This kind of head cannot nod.

More intricate controls involve a lever and fulcrum within the puppet body to transmit a movement from the operator's hand to a part of the puppet, such as eyes, mouth, neck, or fingers. The lever is a manipulated string, wire, or piece of wood; the fulcrum is a nail or screw to which the lever is attached.

Movement of eyes, mouth and eyebrows, nodding, and cocking the head are all built into the main neck rod. This main control rod requires a lot of planning. Do not make the circumference of the neck any larger than the dowel you intend to use for the neck rod. The neck and the rod need to be made for each other. If you prefer, just make the neck extra long, and with your hand inside the puppet body, manipulate the neck rod directly.

A Javanese *Wayang Golek* (rod puppet). This figure comes from the Puppeteerz' collection.

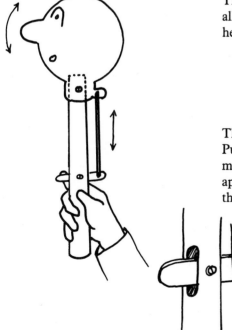

This lever and fulcrum attachment allow a rod puppet to nod its head.

This little lady, made by the Puppeteerz, is opened to show her main control rod. She has appeared on several ring around the collar commercials.

The Control

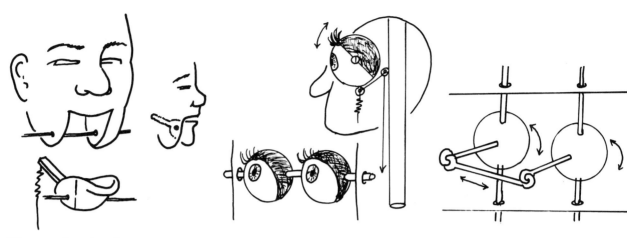

Hinge and spring for a movable mouth on a rod puppet.

These diagrams show the system of springs, wires, and rods needed to control eyes that can open and close.

Rear view of eyes that can move left and right.

The most complicated controls have a combination rod or dowel with a pistol-grip handle. The puppeteer holds the puppet up by the handle and manipulates the dowels and strings with the fingers of the same hand. Almost anything is possible. Some movements, such as moving mouths, rolling, opening, and closing eyes, and wiggling eyebrows and ears are operated by mechanisms built into the main head rod and its handle.

Mechanisms may include rubber bands, springs or counterbalances inside the head. But remember, again, to keep it simple—complicated mechanics do not necessarily make a realistic puppet.

The Head

Like hand puppets, the bottom of the neck must be open to permit the rod to be inserted. For pointers on making simple human puppet heads see chapter two. If you want the puppet's eyes or mouth to move, be sure to leave the crown of the head off until mechanisms are installed (see Margo Rose mold and three-part mold, chapter two).

For a nodding puppet, join the head to the rod with a spring, and with string or cobbler's thread attached to the chin and ears, the puppet will nod and cock its head to either side. The strings pass through a collar attached to the rod and pass to the bottom where the puppeteer pulls them for various movements.

Tiger, showing control. Made by Wayne Lauser.

The neck control on Wayne Lauser's tiger allows the tiger to nod his head and open and close his mouth. These few gestures make a believable tiger puppet. The puppeteer's arm extends up inside the foam rubber body to the neck control, and the legs hang in place.

Some puppeteers hold the head and shoulders up with a short head rod and use one of their own hands as the puppet's hand. These very effective puppets from The Independent Eye company all use this kind of control.
Photographs by G. Grant.

The Torso

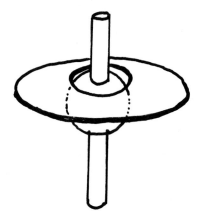

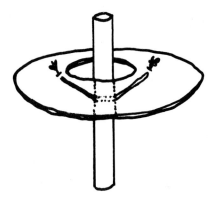

Construction of a movable shoulder joint. Dowel and tennis ball or cord and dowel.

The torso of a rod puppet may be simply suggested. Attach a shoulder-width-long piece of wood at shoulder height, perpendicular to the main support rod. Fabric draped properly over the "shoulders" will create the illusion of a body.

An effective shoulder joint may be created by supporting the wooden shoulder piece on an impromptu universal joint. Skewer a tennis ball on the puppet's main control rod. Carve out a concave area in the shoulder piece and assemble. An alternative is to drill a horizontal hole in the dowel and run a cord through it to either side of the shoulder piece.

To make an upper torso, form some modeling clay and use as a model for a positive mold. Cover the model with layers of papier-mâché, laminated cloth, or Celastic (see chapter two). Leave a hole for the neck rod in the cast. Once you have scooped out the clay mold, you may want to add small wooden braces at the neck and shoulders to support the rod and arms.

To make a full torso, sew and stuff a cloth pattern with polyester or cotton fill. The main rod is inside the soft fabric body, and the stuffing restricts the movement of the head somewhat.

A simple shoulder connection can be made with heavy gauge wire and a wooden spool. Wrap two wires around the circumference of the spool and twist the ends to secure the wires. Loop the ends of the wires back toward the spool and twist them around themselves. Attach arm dowels to these wire loops using eye screws in the dowels.

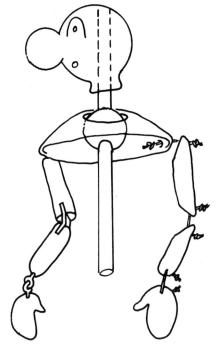

Movable shoulder joint in an assembled rod puppet.

For added effect, Norman Ernsting included padding in the shoulders of this rod puppet.

The wires become the shoulders. The hole in the spool is the neck hole. Because that hole is so small, you will need to sharpen a long nail at both ends. The nail should be longer and skinnier than the spool hole. Pound the head rod onto one end of this double nail, and pound the body rod onto the other end, so that the head is attached above the shoulders, and the puppet is held from below. This leaves the shoulders free to twirl. A costume will cover this simple mechanism and make a very effective rod puppet.

Drape a costume over the chest of just about any rod puppet, and the bottom part of the body will seem sufficiently full. These puppets are from Eric Bass's production of *Maya*. Photograph by Tseng Kwong Chi.

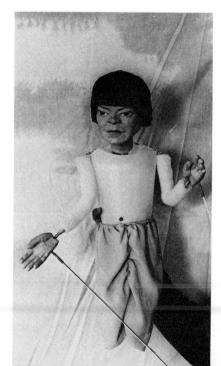

Durable rod puppet bodies can be made of sheets or bottles of polyvinyl plastic, such as this puppet made by Wayne Lauser.

The Arms

Rod puppet arms are, for the most part, identical to marionette arms. Some puppeteers carve muscles and give the elbows sophisticated joints. But in some cases, arms are not even necessary. A puppet hand, which is controlled by a single rod, may be attached to the hem of the garment. When this is done the puppet seems to have very definite arms without all the work of making them. This technique can be used for medieval monks, magicians, and wizards.

If you would like your puppet to have more prominent arms, carve the shape out of a long piece of foam rubber. With a long needle, run some doubled cobbler's thread through the entire length of the foam. Tie one end to the shoulder and the other end to the hand.

You can also use cloth. Sew a tube of cloth with a length and diameter appropriate to the puppet size. Invert so that the seam side is in. Run a triple line of stitches perpendicular to the length of the arm where the elbow should be. Stuff both ends of the tube with cotton or polyester fill. Gather and sew ends, tucking edges in. On the inside portion of the elbow, sew a short tab of cloth to prevent the arm from bending the wrong way at the elbow. With cobbler's thread, tie one end to the shoulder and the other end to a hand.

More difficult to make but longer lasting arms are made of wooden dowels, with standard marionette joints built in. Cut dowels to lengths suitable for forearms and upper arms and join these with small eye screws dipped in glue. Attach the arm to the hand and shoulder with eye screws. For similar limbs, see chapter six.

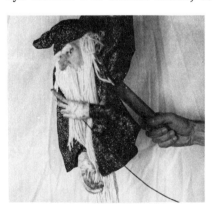

This wizard is a good example of a mechanically simple puppet that is capable of seemingly complicated gestures and various roles.

98

Hands for marionettes, rod puppets and hand puppets are made exactly the same way. The only difference is in the way they are attached to the puppet.

You can make little mittens from felt and stuff them. A variation on this is to cut the mittens out of felt and glue them together with cardboard in between. Or sew the mittens over an armature of wire in the shape of the mitten. Then attach the hands to the rod puppet's arms, providing for the hand rod to be attached to the mitten.

To make a more permanent hand, roll out a pancake of plastic wood, ⅓ to ½ inch thick. Cut out a mitten or hand pattern. Using modeling clay as a brace, shape the hands into the gesture you want and set aside to dry. Before they are completely dry, cut a slot for a hand rod in the heels of the hand. After several hours, remove the modeling clay brace, turn over, and allow other side to dry. The hands can be sanded and finished. Large hands should be coated with Celastic or papier-mâché.

Rods that control the hands are small and can be made of thin dowels, umbrella spokes, bicycle spokes, etc. Attach the rods to the hands with wire, string or a small nail (bent over). Cold rolled steel wire, flattened at one end with a hammer and drilled near the tip for attaching, makes a good hand rod. Handles can be affixed to the bottom, but because hand rods are often manipulated by one hand, the handles might get in the way.

Wayne Lauser made a simple main support rod that holds the puppet up and allows her head to turn and nod. Plugs at the ends of the arm rods allow the operator to operate the hands with his thumb and little finger. This gives him the freedom to operate two rod puppets with the ease usually needed for a hand puppet.

This Iroquois figure, made by Norman Ernsting, hides one of the arm control rods with a cane.

Pickwick Puppets' Alice in Wonderland.

The Legs

Single-hand rod puppet control made by Wayne Lauser.

Legs in rod puppets are often suggested. Since the puppeteer has only two hands, and the puppet has one rod for the head and two for the hands, the kind of movement you can build in is limited. That is why Bunraku puppets sometimes require three puppeteers to manipulate: one to manipulate the head and right arm, one for the body and left arm, and another for the legs. In most rod puppets the legs are left to dangle or are hidden by long robes, dresses or frock coats. Simply attach them to a stuffed cloth apron hung from the front of the body piece.

If you decide to make legs, use the same materials as in the arms (see above), and joint them in the same way. Remember that legs are thicker than arms.

Some rod puppet legs are controlled by wires attached to the main rod and manipulated by the puppeteer's thumb or fingers. But the movement of these legs more closely resembles kicking than walking. Puppets "walk" better without moving their legs.

Paul Vincent-Davis's Samurai Swordsman was patterned after the Japanese Bunraku figures for The Puppet Showplace. Photograph by Alonso.

Legs in rod puppets are often suggested. Eric Bass's O'Neill has legs, but they do not have control rods attached to them. Photograph by Tseng Kwong Chi.

6

MARIONETTES

This is an elf made by Pam and Iver Johnson for their Fool on the Hill Company.

The great advantage of the marionette is that it is almost completely removed from the puppeteer. These Eloi, fanciful creatures from H.G. Wells' imagination, are from the Bennington Puppets production of *The Time Machine*.

The marionette is a puppet manipulated with a combination of strings, wires, or rods attached to a hand-held control above the puppet. The most important characteristics of these puppets are their ability to portray the complete figure from head to toe, and their ability to move very freely. They can fly, dance, stand on their heads, literally fall apart and reassemble themselves or magically transform themselves from one being to another before an audience's eyes. This freedom of movement, however, also makes the marionette the most difficult kind of puppet to control. Because the marionette is the freest of all puppets, movement *restrictions* have to be built in.

Marionettes have been referred to as nothing more than "pendulums with limbs." Ideally, a marionette should do all the work with the aid of gravity and the pendulum effect, while the puppeteer just holds on. In the perfect stringed puppet, the center of gravity of each piece of the puppet is taken into account, which really is not as hard as it sounds. Most puppet heads, for instance, are held up by strings attached to eye screws at either side of the head. If you place these eye screws too far toward the back of the head, the puppet will stare at its feet; if you place them too far forward, it will look up at the puppeteer. But if you place the eye screws in the middle of the head (at its center of gravity), the puppet will look at its audience.

The balancing point of the body, or its two parts, is also easy to find. And in most puppets, the balancing point of the arms, legs and extremities is not critical, especially if both parts of the arms and legs are the same length and weight. If you want the hand to be palm up, attach string to the palm; if you want it palm down, attach it to the back of the hand; and if you want it palm out, attach it to the top edge.

If a puppet is too heavy, the puppeteer tires easily and quickly. If it is too light, it is hard to control because the slightest breeze can move it. A good median weight for a puppet is about four pounds (1.8 Kg). A good median size can range from 12″ (30.5 cm) up to 30″ (76.2 cm).

The modeling, molding and casting of heads has been dealt with in chapter two. The only specific alteration that is recommended for a marionette is to make the bottom of the neck rounded to fit in the neck cavity better.

The Head

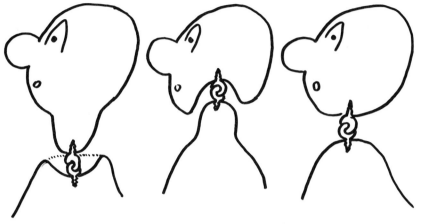

Make the bottom of a marionette neck rounded to fit the neck cavity in the puppet's torso. Shown here are three possible ways of attaching a head to the body of a puppet.

These exquisitely carved basswood marionettes by David Syrotiak demonstrate the simple beauty of the second method of attaching the head to the body of a puppet. Photographs by National Marionette Theatre Studio.

This creature of the Wildwood Marionette Theater is also carved out of basswood and demonstrates how easy it is to cover up the neck joint in a marionette. Photographs by Ted Decever.

Making the Body

The Torso

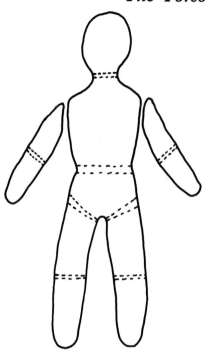

Shape for a sewn and stuffed marionette body. Joints are made by sewing at the dotted lines. The hands and feet need to have extra weight added.

The easiest way to make a torso is with a tube of cloth, tailored to the proper scale and proportions, and filled with polyester or cotton fill. Victorian puppets routinely had cloth bodies with arms, legs, and heads made of wood or some other solid material. Of course the arms and legs can also be made of stuffed cotton or polyester, or the arms, legs and body could be sewn out of one continuous pattern. Since Styrofoam and foam rubber are too light to control well, do not use them for the puppet body unless you weight them.

A variation on the cloth tube body, is a cloth tube tacked and/or glued to three horizontal sections of ½" (1.3 cm) wood (sections at shoulders, waist and hips). The sections define the shape and provide needed weight, and the cloth tube does not require any fill.

Another simple body is cut out of wood with a band saw, coping saw or jigsaw. To articulate the torso, cut it horizontally at the navel and attach the chest piece to the pelvis piece with eye screws. This allows it to do sit-ups.

A clay torso may be modeled in one or two pieces. Cover a positive Plasticene mold with papier-mâché, glue-dipped cloth, or Celastic. Cut the casting apart and remove from the mold. Reassemble and cover seams with papier-mâché, glue-dipped cloth or Celastic. **Please observe the safety precautions recommended for use with these substances.**

A torso model can also be hand sawed and carved of wood. The

Left:
Wooden body pieces.

Right:
Wooden limbs joined by rope, on a cast torso.

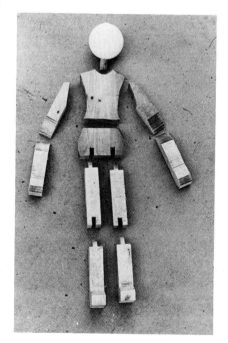

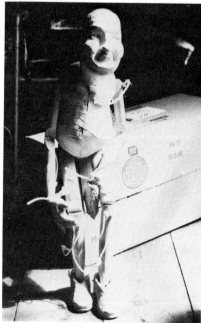

Two piece wooden torso model.

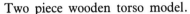

Celastic casts from wooden torso.

Assembled cast torso next to wooden model. Leather loops are threaded through the Celastic body.

wooden pieces are covered with aluminum foil (as a mold release) and then covered with Celastic. As soon as the Celastic is dry, the castings are slit all the way around and removed from the wooden molds. Then the casting halves are reassembled, and the seams covered with small strips of Celastic. The chest section is joined to the pelvis section with leather loops. (See chapter 2 for more information on Celastic casting.)

The Limbs

Although some puppeteers carve musculature in the arms and legs, most puppets will do well with simple wooden dowels connected at the joints.

The easiest way to join a wooden torso and limbs is with a hook and eye. Make a "hook" by opening an eye screw with a needlenose pliers, threading it through a second eye screw, and closing the "hook." Daub a little white glue on the screw before turning it into a piece. If the joint will be exposed, enclose it in a tube of cloth or chamois to make it fleshlike. Most joints, however, are inside sleeves, trousers, and socks and do not have to be doubly hidden by such a tube of cloth.

A second method of joining is with a cord or small rope (rawhide shoelaces and plastic clothesline cord are not recommended). Bevel off adjoining ends of pieces (forearm to arm, thigh to leg) to about a third

Making the Body

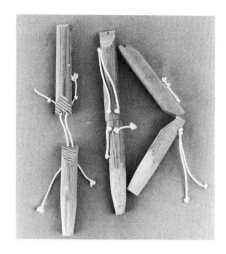

of the thickness. When abutted, the beveled ends should form a wide-angled V. Drill two holes in both top and bottom of joint. Insert line through holes and knot the ends. The knots, in most puppets, will be covered by costumes. This method works well for elbows and knees.

A third way to join parts is with hinges, which are available at hobby and hardware stores. Bevel adjoining ends of pieces. Screw hinges to the inclined planes of the bevel. If you attach the hinge wrong side out, it will hold at a ninety degree angle, so make certain the hinge can fold all the way back like a realistic joint.

Leather straps also make viable joints. Like leather shoelaces, they tend to stretch, wear and break in professional companies due to extensive use, but they work well under less strain. Start with the beveled dowels (as used in rope joints). Parallel to the plane of the bevel, at the point where the bevel meets the end of the dowel, saw a lengthwise slit deep enough to hold a leather strap about ½" to ¾" (1.3 cm to 1.9 cm). Insert the leather strap into the slit. Tack, do not glue, the strap. When leather wears and is ready to be changed, it is easier to remove tacks than glue.

Hinged joints. Cuts; leather joint; tongue and groove joint; rope joint.

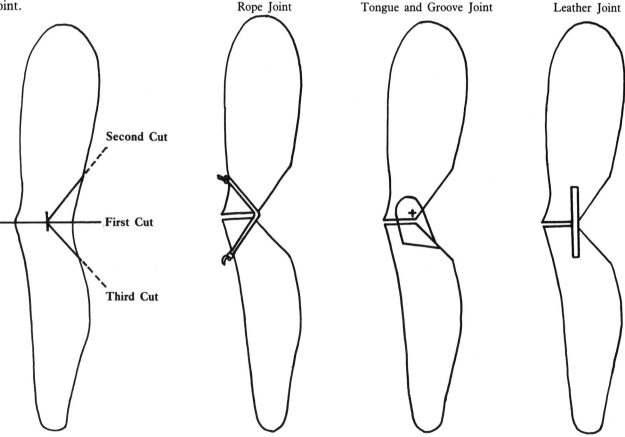

Trunk fiber or polyvinyl plastic sheets can also be used in a durable joint. Instead of cutting a slit at the edge of the bevel, cut it from the front of the knee to the back. Cut one edge of the trunk fiber or plastic into a modified hourglass shape. Slip the fiber or plastic into the slit. Attach it to the lower limb with three brads and to the top limb with one brad (for a pivot). Although simple beveled edges work, the joint can be refined by shaping the bevels more gracefully.

A tongue and groove joint requires some skill. Instead of using a trunk fiber tongue as in the preceding, create a tongue out of wood in the top dowel and a groove for the tongue in the bottom dowel. Round or bevel the abutting dowels or leave them simple planes. Once the tongue is properly shaped and rounded to move properly, attach it to the grooved piece with a single brad.

A more elaborate joint is the ball-and-socket (and fiber) joint. First cut a slot from side to side for trunk fiber or plastic. Round the bottom of one dowel, and with a butterfly drill hollow a round basin in the adjoining dowel. Form the rounded dowel so that it can bend in a realistic way. Affix trunk fiber to the bottom (hollowed) part of the joint with three brads. Fit the ball into the socket over the trunk fiber and affix with one brad for a pivot.

Hands and Feet

In the chapters on modeling and carving, molds and casting, and rod puppets, you will find procedures for making hands and feet that are applicable to marionette hands and feet. If the marionette's hands have individual fingers, sew (or glue) a piece of cobbler's thread through the tips of thumbs and fingers. This will prevent the fingers from getting caught in the strings.

Assembling the Body

Most marionettes are made up of fifteen body pieces. Choosing a method to assemble a marionette depends on the materials being used. If both arms and body are wooden, a glue-dipped hook and eye joint will do.

If the body is Celastic, and the arm is wood, a simple joint that also attaches the head is possible. Drill a hole at the top of the arm, through the shoulder into the neck cavity and back out the other side and through the other arm. Thread a cord (Venetian blind cord is fine)

Making the Body

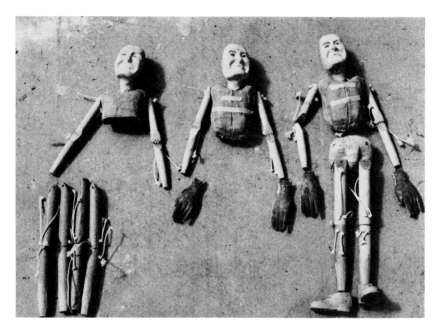

Puppet arms which are tubes of cloth, and a body of Celastic.

The fifteen pieces of most marionettes: a head, two parts of the body, two parts of each arm, two parts of each leg and two hands and two feet.

through the arm, through the shoulder and into the neck cavity, through two holes in the base of the neck, back through the other shoulder, and to the top of the other arm. Knot the cord outside the arms at the shoulder.

If the puppet body is wooden, drill a hole in the neck cavity. Twist an eye screw into the bottom of the neck and insert the eye end of the screw into the hole in the neck cavity. Pound a nail from front to back in the chest through this eye screw. This head will have very reasonable head movements.

Legs can be attached to the pelvis with a nail pushed through holes drilled, side to side, in the legs and in the center of the pelvis piece. The head of the nail keeps one leg from sliding off, and a bend in the nail tip keeps the other leg in place.

Or tack one end of a piece of cloth to the top of the leg and the other end to the bottom of the torso. This is an easy way to assemble the puppet but gives the legs a bit more freedom than necessary. Whereas human legs are capable of lateral movements, as in jumping jacks, lateral movement is unnecessary and in fact undesirable in puppets because it makes legs harder to control.

If the puppet arms are tubes of cloth, and the body is Celastic or a larger tube of cloth, they can simply be sewn together. Make sure the arm can swing a full 360 degrees at the shoulder.

The Strings

A very simple human-figure puppet requires seven strings (one for each side of the head, one each to the hands and feet, and one to the back), but some have as many as forty. Some simple bird puppets can get by with one or two strings.

The first requirement of the string is that it be strong enough to bear the weight of the puppet. In some cases, rods and wires can be used for special effects. Some puppeteers use braided fisherman's nylon string because it is black. Some use Dacron, claiming that nylon stretches. Some use black cobbler's thread to make the strings seem to disappear, while others use white string to draw attention to the puppet's puppetness. Your choice of string depends on what is available, and what your needs are.

Although strings can be tied securely to the control, it is wise to leave open the possibility of adjusting the strings. One way is to cut a slot in the tips of the bars, pull the string through, wrap the string around the bar several times, and pull it down through the slot again. This makes a permanently secured string that is, when necessity arises, adjustable.

A continuous string is one that is attached to matching puppet parts (say, hands), and passes through eye screws or holes in the control.

Because Orlando Furioso marionettes weigh up to seventy-five pounds, their "strings" are two steel rods, one connected directly to top of head, the other to the sword hand.

Some puppeteers, such as Pam and Iver Johnson in their production of Faust, use highly visible strings in order to emphasize the fact that these are puppets.

If the strings are unobtrusive, they tend to vanish in the audience's eyes once the puppet begins to move, as do the strings on this puppet made by Daniel Llords. Photograph by Turner and Jones.

The Control

There are three major types of marionette controls: the horizontal, vertical and pallette control. There is also a simple method of looping continuous strings over the puppeteer's hands, which is still used effectively in India.

The horizontal control (also known as an airplane control or two-hand control), is commonly used in America, where it originated. It is a device made of door sill or slats of wood about 1½" (3.8 cm) wide and ¼" (.6 cm) thick, joined in the rough shape of an airplane.

The removable front bar is attached to strings leading to the legs. The permanently attached rear bar is connected with strings to eye screws in the side of the head. A continuous string passes through two eye screws in the front and is attached to both hands. Another continuous string passes through two eye screws in the middle of the main bar and connects with the shoulders. And a single string connects the back end of the bar with the back of the marionette (for bowing).

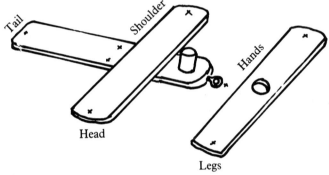

The horizontal control.

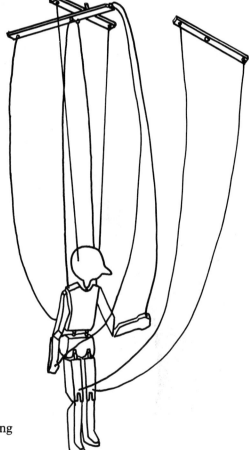

Horizontal control and stringing pattern for marionette.

The Control

By holding the main bar in one hand, and the front bar in the other, the puppeteer can make the puppet walk. An infinite variety of actions is possible when the puppeteer pulls at individual strings with the fingers of one hand or the other.

A variation of the two-hand control is the one-hand control. The detachable front wings are attached above the main bar on a second bar with two-inch lengths of cord. By wobbling the top bar, the puppeteer can walk the puppet with only one hand; the rest of the strings are connected to the lower plane which hangs relatively stationary.

In addition to the standard control strings, add extra screws and strings to control such movements as rolling the eyes, lifting the elbows and opening the mouth. Every puppeteer will develop unique controls to suit the complexity of movement required by the puppet.

The vertical control, European in origin, is like the horizontal control, except the "airplane" is flying straight up. The front bar is still attached to the legs, while the back bar is attached to head and hands with a continuous string. Some vertical controls have a back bar rising out from the main bar to provide a back string for bowing. Variations of the vertical control have as many as four different wings with numerous strings attached and a pivoting front control to allow the puppeteer to walk the puppet with one hand.

A third control is the palette control, developed by William A. Dwiggins. His tiny (a little over 6″ or 15.2 cm) control is shaped like a sweep-wing aircraft and makes the subtlest movements in 12″ (30.5 cm) puppets. On the wing are strings for the head, forearm, and hands. On the main bar are strings for the forehead, shoulders, and back. The legs are controlled by a small piece of wood, vertical to the main bar and fixed on a pivot so the puppeteer can control the legs simply by rocking the bar with a finger.

Dwiggins' control embodies an important principle: the control should be hand sized. There is little advantage in making the controls big because they have to fit the hand of the operator. It is better to make them as small as possible while still retaining necessary leverage. Thought should be given to providing as many automatic movements as possible simply by tilting the control. But, as usual, keep it as simple as possible.

There are also multiple controls for operating more than one puppet at a time and trick controls for special effects. Trick controls are made by puppeteers to suit their needs. The control is, in a way, half the puppet and must be as flexible as the puppet itself.

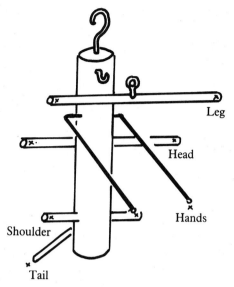

The vertical control.

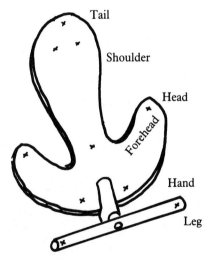

The paddle control, after William A. Dwiggins.

The Control

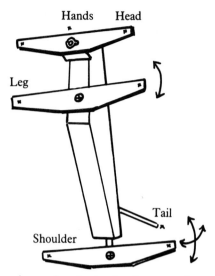

A one-hand pistol grip control, after Albrecht Roser.

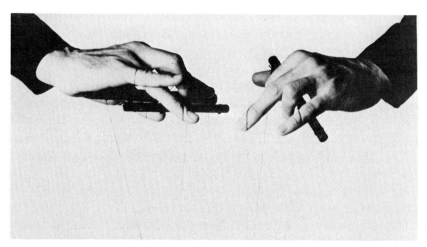

Daniel Llords has spent a lifetime in puppetry, and he knows that the control should fit in your hand. Here is one of his hand-sized controls. Photograph by Turner and Jones.

Stringing the Puppet

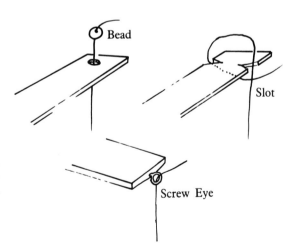

Methods for securing marionette strings to the control.

When you have completed the marionette, including costume and make-up (painting), and have constructed the control, you are ready for stringing the puppet. Although this can be a one-person job, it is easier with two. A stand can be helpful, so you can hang the puppet while attaching strings. Costuming the puppet, too, can be fairly easy if the puppet is hanging.

As you attach the strings, be certain that your puppet is standing on the floor. All of the strings should be about the same tension, except the shoulder strings. These should be a bit more taut.

● Hold the control at the height needed for a performance. If the puppeteer is going to stand on the same floor as the puppet, hold it at chest level. If the puppeteer is going to be on a bridge, string the puppet from there. Tie the string, with a square knot, to a small eye screw attached to one shoulder; pass the string through eye screws in the belly of the control back down to another small eye screw in the other shoulder, and square knot it. This string bears the major weight of the puppet.

- Attach strings to the sides of the head, making a permanent (though adjustable) connection to the control. These should not be as taut as the shoulder strings.
- Attach the back string. Do not make it too tight, or the puppet will have a permanent bow.
- Attach a continuous string from one puppet hand, up through eye screws in the control, and back down to the other hand. String should be slack enough to allow the arms to hang at the side, but not so loose that they will tangle easily. Attach the leg strings to the knees. Each knee gets one string that is permanently fixed to the foot bar (also adjustable).

The single most common problem with marionettes is tangled strings. The secret to keeping them untangled is to keep them taut. You can do this by hanging the puppets by the control with their feet off the ground when they are not in use. If you are taking your show on the road, twirl the puppet around, wrapping the strings in a spiral around each other and keeping the strings taut. Then wrap the twirled strings around the main bar of your control. If this does not keep the strings from tangling, remember that the worst that can happen is that you will have to restring the marionette.

Jim Gamble and his puppets. The length of the strings will vary according to where the puppet will perform, as shown in this photo of Jim Gamble with one of his short-string marionettes.

This device, used to hang puppets for stringing or costuming, is made with angle braces.

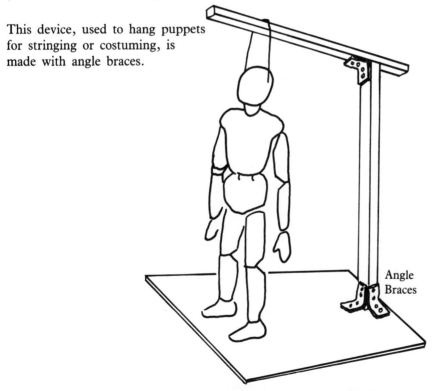

Angle Braces

7

STAGING
AND
PAINTING

Little Red Riding Hood and the Wolf, created by Don Ave for Puppets with a Purpose. Photograph by Professional Photographic Services.

Almost anything—a doorway, a chair, a box—can be used for a puppet stage. However, there is no law that says a puppeteer must be hidden, so stages are not even necessary. It all depends on the puppeteer's needs.

Jean Mattson as Gordo the Clown with Poppy in *Me and My Flea*, a puppet circus show. Photograph courtesy Seattle Puppetory Theatre.

Hand Puppets

Anything that has an edge and a place to hide a puppeteer—such as a window, a clipped hedge, a neighbor's fence—can be turned into a hand puppet stage. Even a wheelchair can have a small, simple stage attached.

Set a table on its edge, sit on the floor behind it, and perform at the edge of the tabletop. With some folding tables, you can leave the top two legs folded out of the way. Try placing two card tables on end, side by side, or four in a square. If you use six in a hexagon, you can make a puppet's version of a theater in the round.

Another possibility is to use a folding screen of either three or four panels zig-zagged or formed into a square U or box. Puppeteers stand behind or in it, and the puppets perform on the top edge.

If none of these things is available, you can always tack a blanket halfway up a doorway. The blanket hides the puppeteers, and the puppets perform on the top edge. Or secure a broom handle to the top of two chairs, or between two step ladders, and drape a blanket over the dowel. Puppeteers hide behind the blanket and the puppets perform at the top edge of the blanket.

Stage Construction

Create an impromptu stage by placing your puppeted hand through the crook of your other arm.

Blanket and door for a hand puppet stage.

For a more elaborate stage, cut a square hole in a panel of a large cardboard box. With the hole at the top it is a stage for hand puppets. Turn this same theater upside down, and it is a stage for marionettes. Add curtains if you wish.

A more permanent hand puppet theater can be made with three 4' × 8' (1.2 m × 2.4 m) panels of light plywood. Hinge the 8' (2.4 m) edges at ninety-degree angles to form three sides of a box. A stage is cut out of the center panel. The height of this hole is determined by the reach of the shortest puppeteer and whether or not the puppeteers plan to stand, sit on the floor, or sit on benches or chairs. Several stages can be cut out of the center panel, or any panel for that matter. Secure the shape of the unfolded stage with a brace, add curtains on a pull string, install lighting, and decorate the panels appropriately. The panels can also be made of pressboard, chipboard, Masonite or anything else the puppeteer can find and cut through.

In ancient China, hand puppeteers walked around in "bag theaters." They made small, light stages out of wood, which were held above them by supports to the shoulders and encircled with a bag of cloth to hide the puppeteer within. A converted trailer home can also make a very effective traveling professional stage.

A box with a square cut out becomes a stage two ways.

The size of your stage need not limit your imagination. Here the Ha Ha Puppet Theatre's giant joins other soft-sculpted hand puppets in *The Bubble Bush*. Photograph by Lionel J-M Delevigne.

Determine stage height by the expected height of the puppeteer.

Stage Construction

A self-contained "bag theater" for puppets.

In Black Box puppetry, the puppeteer is not hidden from the audience but is clothed in black, against a black background. Stage lights shine down on the puppets, leaving the puppeteer in the shadows and effectively removing the puppeteer from the scene.

A variation on this theme is Black Light Puppetry. Black light is a filtered, long-wave Ultra Violet light, a form of radiant energy just beyond the range of human vision. The puppet is painted and dressed in material that reflects this light in fluorescent form. The puppeteer, wearing black, disappears.

Black box puppetry.

Traveling puppet companies may turn a trailer home into an elaborate stage, such as this one of the Gingerbread Players. Photograph by John Gaydos.

Rod Puppets

Practically any stage devised for hand puppets can be used without alteration for rod puppets. Many modern hand puppets, for example, such as those seen on Sesame Street and the Muppets Show, are combination rod and hand puppets and are very much at home on the same stage.

The only modification recommended in more permanent rod puppet theaters is the holding rail—a slotted rail fixed to the edge of the puppet stage window. This is also called a play board. Control rods can be inserted into the holding rail so the puppets can "stand" in place while the puppeteer manipulates other parts of the puppet or other puppets. This helps in crowd scenes. In advanced rod puppet stages, holding rails are installed at several depths in the playing area to give versatility in blocking out the action.

Marionettes

The most complicated of puppets usually demand the most complicated stages, especially if the puppeteer is to be hidden. The practice of hiding the puppeteer began in Victorian times when secrecy in puppetry was the vogue. However, this practice is unnecessary. Many puppeteers perform fully visible, and most people in the audience do not seem to mind. Although the puppets are most important, the dance a puppeteer goes through during a performance is also well worth watching.

A simple stage can be patterned after those in India. It is made quickly and packs away easily. Simply tack a blanket to each side of a door frame, stand behind the blanket, and have the performance on the floor in front of it.

Some marionette puppeteers perform above the stage area on a catwalk, or even several catwalks, affixed to the top of some scenery, such as trees, columns, or buildings. The puppeteers may be in full view of the audience or may be hidden behind a front panel. Some even use hydraulically controlled cherry pickers. These advanced stages require much planning and advanced carpentry skills, not to mention money and determination. To construct them, far more advanced books than this should be consulted. For information on shadow puppet stage construction, see chapter three.

Blanket and door for a marionette stage.

Stage Construction

Puppeteers may control marionettes while in full view of the audience.

Painting the Stage

Painting a stage can be simple or complex, depending on the artistic skills of those who are painting.

A sheet of white or manila paper may carry a scene painted with acrylics or water colors. This can be very effective. If strong lights will shine on the scenery, the colors have to be especially vibrant to prevent their being "washed out" by the stage lights.

Scenery may be painted on wooden boards or a piece of plywood, using regular enamel paints. Stage flats can be made of canvas stretched on a frame. Curtains, with details cut in, appliquéd on, painted on, or just pinned to them, may be pulled down over another flat for a quick scenery change. Some puppeteers make whole stage sets with minature trees, tables, chairs, and cars, using any of the many materials suggested for the making of puppets. Paints should be compatible with the material used to construct the props or sets.

Stage lights of different colors will alter the painted scenery. A little planning and practice will enable you to take advantage of this, varying the mood by changing the lighting. Other than that, the painting of scenery is much like the painting of a picture, be it a landscape or a still life or an interior scene. You can make scenery as realistic or as free form as you choose, depending on its purpose in your production.

A well-painted outdoor stage front for Saint Ann's Episcopal School in Brooklyn. Photograph by Cedric Flower.

Painting the Finished Puppet

Since puppets are born actors, they naturally have a stage make-up complexion. For the most professional results, consult books on theatrical make-up. But for most puppets, all that is needed is imagination and a little knowledge of paint.

Painting is useful not only to help bring out the puppet's features, but to cover any flaws in its making. By making use of the optical illusions suggested by color, you can, to some extent, correct structural weaknesses or alter the shape of the face simply by applying the proper paint.

Paint can add character to a puppet's face. This expressive Cenerentola was made for Seattle Puppetory Theatre's production of the old Italian Cinderella story. Photograph courtesy Seattle Puppetory Theatre.

Paint and Its Uses

All paint consists of three elements: 1) a vehicle, such as water or oil, which evenly spreads a 2) pigment over the surface being painted, and 3) a binder or adhesive to keep the thin film of pigment from flaking off once the vehicle has evaporated or dried. Paints, or more precisely their vehicles, must be compatible with the surfaces they are to cover or abut. For example, use flexible paints on flexible surfaces (glossy enamels, which are not flexible, will flake at the first stretch of a rubber puppet's mouth or wiggle of its nose).

There are three kinds of paint: 1) petroleum-based paints, such as lacquer, 2) oil-based paints, such as enamels, which require thinners, and 3) water-based paints, such as temperas, acrylics, and latexes, which are the safest, easiest and most commonly used. These three kinds of paint are not compatible with each other.

Lacquers and Oil-Based Paints

Oils, which come in tubes, are the longest lasting colors and take the longest to dry, but the effects you can achieve, with talent and patience, can be extraordinary. Introductory kits include anywhere from six to twelve colors, and a mixing guide will give you access to 140 different tones and hues using eight basic colors. You will need linseed oil, thinner, a palette, palette knife, cup and, to speed things along, a quick-drying medium mixed into the paint itself. For cleaning up, you need gum turpentine, linseed oil, a shellac thinner, or a mineral-spirits solvent. **Use caution when handling these fluids.**

Regular enamels can be used to paint puppets, but, again, you will need turpentine for thinning and clean-up. They come in liquid form in a variety of colors and have either glossy or matte finishes.

Lacquers are the hardest, most durable of available paints. They are best applied by spraying, and leave a glasslike sheen.

Some puppeteers will want to try lacquers and oil paints for the qualities which can be found no other way. **For school and home puppet construction, the complications of these paints and their hazardous thinners may outweigh the advantages. Water-based paints are recommended for most puppet makers.**

Water-Based Paints

Watercolors that come in sets of small cakes are generally a little too pale for most puppets. But watercolors that come in tubes produce pastel and opaque colors, and they are very safe and easy to use.

Tempera paints are also safe and easy to use. They come in cakes, plastic jars, powder form, and squeeze bottles (one of which is used like a marker). They come in many colors, including fluorescent and psychedelic shades, and they mix easily and dry quickly to a smooth, velvety finish. A final coat of shellac, varnish or plastic spray acrylic is recommended to prevent chipping and flaking.

Acrylic and latex paints are widely-used, water-based paints. They work well on most surfaces, even on Styrofoam and foam rubber. They can be thinned with water and thickened with talc or gesso to an impasto thickness, which reduces the gloss finish. They come in many colors in tubes, cartridge dispensers, cans and plastic jars. Acrylic and latex paints dry quickly, so second coats can be applied almost immediately. Some are also nontoxic and safe to use. Apply a coat of gesso (available at art supply stores) and let the gesso dry before you paint your puppet.

The puppet head at left has an undercoat of gesso. The head at right has its base color for a caucasian face.

Painting the Finished Puppet

Application

Do not wander too far off the base color when applying any of the shadings.

Most puppeteers apply highlights and lowlights with a regular paintbrush. You can also use small sponges (or sponge brushes found in hardware stores) to dab one color over another. Or you can stipple the colors, using two short bristle brushes to punch at the surface, and making a "pointillism" mix of the colors.

A caucasian human puppet face is painted in four shades. The first shade is an undercoat, or base color, similar to a caucasian complexion. It is a mixture of white with yellow (4:1) with a touch of burnt sienna and orange. Once the base color is applied, use the other three shades sparingly, so that the face will not look artificial. The second shade, light shadow, requires mixing a little blue with the base color. The third shade, lowlight, is made by mixing even more blue into the base color. And the final shade is the highlight, made by adding white to the base color.

A light-shadow shade is used for the side of the nose, indentation of the upper lip, and sides of the head. The lowlight shade is used for deeper shadows in pronounced folds and wrinkles in the face, under the eyebrows, eyes, nose, pronounced cheek bones and chin.

A highlight shade used on the bridge of the nose, cheek planes, crown of the head (if bald), forehead, and chin. Both lowlight and highlight shadings are worked into the base color and smoothed out slightly.

Applying the highlight to a puppet's face.

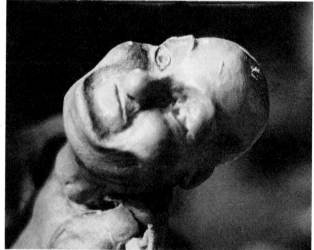

A bright light shows the shadows which a puppet's face will have under stage lights.

A combination of overhead lights and footlights is used in normal stage lighting. The crown of the puppet's head, the forehead, the line of the nose, and the plane of the cheeks and chin receive the most light when the puppet is on stage. The hollows of the cheeks, the sides of the temples, the undersides of the eyebrow ridge, the lower eyelid, and the chin are all left in varying degrees of shadow. Keep this in mind as you experiment with light and dark shades in painting your puppet.

Painting the shadowed areas too light and the lighted areas too dark will result in a flat and expressionless face. By painting the shadowed areas darker and the lighted areas lighter, the face becomes well defined and often striking.

Stage lighting can affect the color of a face as well. Pink, for instance, looks grey and colorless under green lights. Warm colors (yellows) appear closer, while cold colors (blues) appear farther away than neutral colors (reds and greens). Pale colors assume the quality of

Left:
The expression on a puppet's face can be altered by lighting the puppet from below, rather than from above. Here is the apprentice who has forgotten the spell, from Penny Jones and Company Puppets' production of *The Magic Forest.* Photograph by David Kreindler.

Right:
When painting a puppet's face, prepare for the effects of stage lighting. Features and feelings remain clear, here, as one of David Syrotiak's marionettes faces the spotlight. Photograph by National Marionette Theatre Studio.

Painting the Finished Puppet

the background. Colors not mixed with black, white or grey, which are neutralizers, stand out in the foreground.

A caucasian flesh tone can be approximated by *underpainting:* applying the highlights and lowlights over the base color in layers that are translucent enough to allow the base color to show through. This is done by applying the highlights and lowlights in thin washes and gives the skin tone a depth very like natural skin. It is a technique developed by the masters in oil painting and is recommended for advanced students of puppetry.

Traditional Coloration

Do not imitate the natural colors of human faces. The make-up of the puppet, like that of the live actor, is a result of the art of exaggerated contrasts and highlights. In old faces, shadows and shades are accentuated by browns and pale greens. Young faces use warmer shades of red like vermillion and sometimes orange in the base color with lowlights added by blues and purples.

White should not be used for eyes; it makes them appear flat. Combine white with a little blue or grey. To make them sparkle, add a fake jewel for the pupil. Shellac or lacquer the eyes and lips to liven up the expression of the face.

For other races, colors can be added to the basic caucasian (a color called "flesh" is available). For instance, a Chinese face needs a little more white and a touch of yellow; a Japanese face, a very little burnt sienna to lean toward tan; native Americans, white, a little red, and burnt sienna; and, a black person, burnt sienna with black for lowlights and white for highlights.

Nasty witches are traditionally a combination of hideous greens, evil people are highlighted in oranges and lowlighted in blues, over a base of pea green, and the indigent are often painted in greys and purples with shades of yellow and brown.

Under stage lighting, the slightly pronounced shadings and highlights seem to fade, and the face becomes a rather realistic representation of a human face. The hair, mustaches and costumed body complete this narrator for the Bennington Puppets' production of *The Time Machine.*

8

PUPPETRY
IN
EDUCATION

Puppets are useful in the classroom because they are fun—and they make learning fun. They are special little beings over whose lives even children can exercise control. Puppets are also magic. With strings, wires, rods or a hand, they come to life and assume an independent personality.

A scene from *Mother Goose Tales*, performed by Penny Jones and Company Puppets. Photograph by David Kreindler.

Puppets as Teachers

For centuries, puppets have combined their magic with education. The legendary Chiao-meng used the magical effects of his puppet to instruct Emperor Wu-ti on matters of state and on being a better ruler. The education program of the Roman Catholic Church extensively involved puppets, as well. And missionaries have often used puppets to teach the tenets of Buddhism, Hinduism, Islam and Christianity. Puppets have been used to enact portions of national or religious epics, such as the *Bible*, the *Mahabharata*, and the *Ramayana*, practically from the time these texts were written. As religious teaching tools, puppets were indispensible because the "students" were often illiterate.

Even when puppets were used for entertainment, they taught lessons through morality plays, fairy tales, myths and legends. The amazing impact of Sesame Street and the Muppets attest that puppets still play an important role as an established teaching tool.

Today, special education programs, hospitals, clinics and the National Committee: Art for the Handicapped use puppets to attract and maintain the attention of children with learning disabilities, physical disabilities, and emotional problems. Both the therapist and

Some puppet shows teach fairy tales such as this Penny Jones and Company version of *Goldilocks and the Three Bears*. Photograph by Michael Hunoldt.

Puppets as Teachers

Barbara Aiello uses her Kids on the Block to teach handicapped children about themselves, and to teach non-handicapped children to understand. Photographs by Barr A. Forrest.

Creator Barbara Aiello with (from left to right) Vallerie Perkins, Mark Riley, Renaldo Rodriguez, Ellen Jane Peterson, Mandy Puccini, and Melody James.

the clients can manipulate puppets. Puppets can succeed in overcoming some of the knottiest problems.

By introducing puppet making in the art room, students can learn sculpting, woodworking, modeling, casting, painting, sewing, mechanics, and the use of tools, design and the imagination. When puppets are finished, they can be taken into the classroom to teach

Nicolas Coppola's marionettes
teach such classic Western music
and literature as *Philomon and
Beaucis,* a Haydn opera, *Peter and
the Wolf,* and *The Magic Flute,* a
Mozart opera.

Body puppets, such as this one
designed by Nancy Renfro Studios
and modeled by Eleanor Click, are
helpful for therapy with deaf,
motor impaired or
multihandicapped people. The
puppeteer's hands are free to use
sign language and body awareness
is amplified. Photograph by Nancy
Renfro studios.

Nancy Renfro produces a puppet
stage which can be clamped to a
wheelchair or bed table.
Photograph by Nancy Renfro
Studios.

self-expression, improvisation, music, singing, speaking, dramatic presentation, scenery painting, stagecraft, creative writing, teamwork and self-confidence.

But puppets are not limited to the art room. Teachers can make current events come to life in students' minds with a cast of hand puppets created from newspapers and magazines. Art teachers are experimenting, discovering and creating programs around the use of puppets by collaborating with teachers, librarians, social service counselors, members of the clergy and just about anyone else to teach students history, languages, literature, sociology, health, nutrition, ecology and personal behavior. Not incidentally, these students are also introduced to an ancient, kinetic, three-dimensional art form they might otherwise have considered "kid's stuff."

Imaginative teachers all over the country are making puppets full partners in presenting lessons. A wise old gnome can be called upon to teach literature. A whale puppet can teach about whale migration and relate it to other ecological facts. A terrible speller from outer space can excite children to learn to spell just to help the little puppet adjust to their world. Personable little creatures who believe in honesty can be very useful in inspiring good social behavior. Children often prefer learning from puppets instead of teachers.

A bird's eye view of history is presented by Ben Jay while Baby Ben listens, in Nancy Renfro's show *Ben Franklin*. Photograph by Nancy Renfro Studios.

A whale and a possum can teach natural history. These two are by Gingerbread Players. Photo by John Gaydos.

Puppets as Therapists

Puppetry is most frequently used to allow students a means of self-expression. The very shy can magically learn to express themselves through small puppets, because the puppets, not the children, are doing the talking. And aggressive children, given a gentle puppet like a butterfly, might learn to modify aggressive behavior.

Another form of self-expression is the venting of frustrations. That is probably Punch's secret: he gives vent to dreams of violence forbidden to most of his young audience. Puppetry is a safe arena in which troubled students can work out their problems and learn valuable (and inexpensive), lessons without inflicting serious damage on themselves and others.

Most therapeutic work is accomplished on a one-to-one basis, with a teacher or counselor helping a child communicate hidden feelings. Puppets are used for reaching the severely handicapped in several ways. A counselor can manipulate a puppet and have the child try to relate to it. (A puppet is less of a threat than anything else the child has ever met, and as long as the little puppet moves, a child will pay attention to it.) Or the child can manipulate a puppet and express hidden or suppressed feelings, fears or ideas through it.

In some typical instances, a brief dramatic presentation is made, showing puppets confronting some problem or expressing some emotion. Then the confrontation or expressed emotion is discussed and problems diagnosed. In a way, it is like "miniaturizing" a problem to make it more manageable for a child. The problem is no longer so big that the child cannot grasp it. There are instances of children with no verbal communications skills relating to puppets, developing those skills, and then being able to use them with adults.

Puppets are little beings with human-sized voices. They are oddly powerful little creatures who are at the same time nonthreatening. A puppet's voice is most effective if it is a bit exaggerated, because an exaggerated voice is easier to identify and more fun to listen to. A puppet can make a funny voice to discipline a child without embarrassment. Puppets are versatile. Use them to teach many subjects in conjunction with books, posters, maps, audio-visual aids, and the arts, and to develop and improve listening habits and general deportment. Puppets can often get and keep a child's attention better than any human being could. They make lessons come alive!

APPENDIX
A
GUIDE
TO
USING
PUPPETS

Some Uses of Puppetry	Types Most Frequently Used	Typical Size	Characteristics	Puppeteer/Staging	Examples
Classroom, Therapy, Library	Hand, rod, shadow	12″ to 24″ high	Close-up puppetry. Audience participation. Dialogue. Soft puppets and well built puppets for use by children. Relatively simple puppets. Hand puppets for holding and demonstrating. Well suited for improvisation, language skills, motor skills, self expression, and academics with fun.	Puppeteer may be student or teacher. Single or group puppeteers in full view or hidden by screens or small booths. Sometimes interaction between puppet and pupil, puppet and teacher or therapist, puppet and audience.	Speech classes, The Kids on the Block, Susan Lynn

Some Uses of Puppetry	Types Most Frequently Used	Typical Size	Characteristics	Puppeteer/Staging	Examples
Theater	Rod, shadow, large marionettes	24" to 6'	Action and movement, scenery and props, storytelling and dramatic exposition. An element of non-puppet theater; e.g. bats in Dracula. An element of non-puppet music; e.g. Stravinski's "Histoire du Soldat."	A full puppet company consists of 3 to 12 puppeteers. Puppet control skills range from beginner to professional. Puppeteers are usually hidden behind elaborate staging. Good acting skills required. Voices or dialogue may be recorded.	Bunraku, Salzburg Marionettes, Bil Baird, Bennington Puppets
Television, Film	Hand, rod, shadow	21" to 30"	Heavy reliance on dialogue. Very mobile faces, mouths and eyes. Puppets often of rubber, fabric and foam. Subtle movements; careful modeling and detail. Strings, Rods and other mechanics not usually visible.	One to three puppeteers per puppet. Camera angle used to hide puppeteer and mechanicals. Chromakey photography sometimes used to hide puppeteer. Voices "live," or "dubbed" at a later time. Puppeteers must be highly skilled.	Muppets, King Kong (stop motion), extra terrestrials, animated cartoons, Pillsbury dough boy
Cabaret	Hand, rod, "short strung" marionettes	6" to 30"	Close-up puppetry. Heavy reliance on dialogue. Trick, novelty, and circus puppetry; jugglers, skaters, slapstick, ventriloquism.	Single puppeteer using one or two puppets. Puppeteer in full view of audience or masked with small booth. Sometimes use of a small recording system for music or sound effects. Voices are "live." Good for outdoor performances. Puppeteers must be highly skilled.	Kookla 'n Ollie, Madam, Punch 'n Judy, Charlie McCarthy
Pageant	Large rod and body puppets	6' and up	Rely on size, shape and color for effect. Must be lightweight, as they are carried or worn. May be choreographed or dance-like.	Large number of puppeteers. Puppets have large but limited movements and do not require advanced skills. Highly effective outdoors.	Bread 'n Puppets, Matawee River Theatre Co., Macy's Parade, Chinese New Year's Dragons

BIBLIOGRAPHY

Baird, Bil. *The Art of the Puppet*. New York: The Macmillan Company, 1965. Toronto: Collier-Macmillan Canada, Ltd., 1965.

Binyon, Helen. *Puppetry Today*. New York: Watson-Guptil Publications Inc., 1966. London: Studio Vista Ltd., 1966.

Creegan, George. *Sir George's Book of Hand Puppetry*. Chicago, New York: Follett Publishing Company, 1966.

Cummings, Richard. *101 Handpuppets: A Guide for Puppeteers of All Ages*. New York: Van Ross Press, 1962.

Dwiggins, William A. *Marionettes in Motion*. Boston: Trustees of Public Library of the City of Boston, 1976. (originally *Puppetry Imprints*, 1939)

Engler, Larry and Fijan, Carol. *Making Puppets Come Alive*. New York: Taplinger, 1973.

Fettig, Hansjürgen. *Glove and Rod Puppets*. Translated by John Wright and Susanne Forster. London: George G. Harrap & Co. Ltd., 1973.

Fling, Helen. *Marionettes: How to Make and Work Them*. New York: Dover Publications, Inc., 1973.

Kraska, Edie. *Toys & Tales from Grandmother's Attic*. New York: Houghton Mifflin & Co., 1979.

Lynch-Watson, Janet. *The Shadow Puppet Book*. New York: Sterling Publishing Co., Inc., 1980.

Philpotl, Violet and McNeil, Mary Jean. *The Fun Craft Book of Puppets*. New York: Scholastic Book Services, 1976.

Ross, Laura. *Hand Puppets: How to Make and Use Them*. New York: Lathrop, 1969.

Simmen, Rene. *The World of Puppets*. New York: Thomas Y. Crowell Company. 1975.

Simon, Bernard, ed. *Simon's Directory of Theatrical Materials, Services and Information*. New York: Package Publicity Service, Inc., 1975. This resource tells where to find many materials useful in puppetry and lists theater-related books, films, agents, organizations, and much more. Revised editions are published as the contents are periodically updated.

Sims, Judy. *Puppets for Dreaming and Scheming: A Puppet Source Book*. Walnut Creek, California: Early Stages Press, Inc., 1978.

Tangerman, E.J. *Design and Figure Carving*. Toronto: General Publishing Company, 1940.

Tichenor, Thomas. *Tom Tichenor's Puppets*. New York: Abington Press, 1971.

Van Gelder, Amy. *Felt Toy Making*. New York: Drake Publishers, 1974.

ORGANIZATIONS

The Puppeteers of America, Inc. is a national non-profit organization dedicated to preserve, promote and develop the art of puppetry in America. Annual conferences are held in different locations throughout the country, usually in June or August. Regional puppetry festivals are held in many major U.S. cities by guilds associated with the parent organization. The Puppeteers of America, Inc., publishes a bi-monthly Puppetry Journal, maintains an audio/visual library and a puppetry store for books and related materials.

For further information contact:

Nancy Lohman Staub
2311 Connecticut Ave., N.W. #501
Washington, D.C. 20008
or

Gayle G. Schulter
#5 Cricklewood Path
Pasadena, California 91107

UNIMA (Union Internationale de la Marionnette) is an organization in which all those people who are concerned with the art of the puppet theatre associate voluntarily. Their aim is to serve through their art the idea of peace and of mutual understanding of peoples, without distinction as to race, political ideas or religion. It was founded in Prague, Czechoslovakia in 1929 and its publications are published in both English and French.

For further information in the U.S.A. contact

Mollie Falkenstein
132 Chiquita Street
Laguna Beach, California 92651
or
Allelu Kurten,
Browning Road
Hyde Park, New York 12538
or

UNIMA—Canada
887 Keith Road
Vancouver, British Columbia
Canada

The Educational Puppetry Association was formed in 1943. For further information write to:

Honorable Secretary
Educational Puppetry Association
The Puppet Center,
Battersea Town Hall Community Arts Centre
Lavender Hill
London SW 11, England

INDEX